Jan 20 2009

TRUE STORIES : REAL PEOPLE : ONE DAY

By 58 Authors on WEbook.com

WEbook, Inc.
307 Fifth Avenue, 7th Floor
New York, NY 10016
646.453.8575
www.WEbook.com

ISBN: 978-1-935003-06-9

Library of Congress Cataloging-in-Publication Data has been applied for.

Printed in the United States.

Contents

Introduction

history is usually made or declared only after the fact. Generally, we don't see it coming. In hindsight, we memorialize tragedies—assassinations of our heroes and entries into our wars. Less often, we look back on the happier milestones—a moon landing, the destruction of the Berlin wall, the founding of a democracy.

Far more rare are the times when we know—in advance—that history will be made on a future date. In those unusual instances, people can make plans—travel, organize a party of friends, or take a sick day. The inauguration of Barack Obama, the 44th President of the United States, on January 20, 2009, was one of those times. Almost two million people watched live in Washington, DC, and hundreds of millions more tuned in across the globe to witness an American event that carried with it global significance for an astounding range of people.

WEbook.com stepped in to create *Jan 20, 2009, a Community-Sourced History*—an unfiltered collection of writing as immediate as the moment it chronicles. The following 60 essays are culled from the work of nearly 200 writers who came together to lend their words to a new kind of historic record. Enabled by WEbook's online platform, *Jan. 20, 2009* tells the stories within the story of Barack Obama's ascent to the Presidency.

The result is a collective "gut reaction" to history that leaves an indelible imprint of a day that surely will be studied for decades and centuries.

The contributions on the pages that follow appear almost exactly as they were submitted to WEbook. Each is a history unto itself, but together they speak volumes about the power of "new media" to get at the marrow of a moment through the eyes of authentic, on-the-ground correspondents.

This kind of collection would not be possible without the lifeblood of WEbook.com—the writers who contribute their words, their feedback, and most of all their time to create innovative new creative works. In tribute to aspiring writers everywhere and in honor of the historic occasion of this writing, all author royalties and WEbook profits from the sale of *Jan. 20, 2009* will go to 826 National, a non-profit tutoring, writing, and publishing organization with locations in seven cities across the U.S. 826 National works to get young people excited about writing. It is our sincere hope that *Jan 20, 2009* does that for you. It certainly did for us.

—The WEbook team

We Will Not Walk with Fear

Tananarive Due

f or me, the experience of Inauguration Day is inextricably tied to my parents.

It was a long walk to the inauguration of Barack Obama for my parents, civil rights attorney John Due and longtime activist Dr. Patricia Stephens Due. On election night, my sisters Johnita, Lydia and I traveled with our families to be with them in Quincy, Florida, and I'll never forget the ecstatic joy from the living room when the words "President-elect Barack Obama" appeared on the television screen—and Obama's smiling face.

To understand the meaning of our long family walk, you have to know where it started.

Both of my parents were college students in 1960, when my mother and her sister, Priscilla, were first arrested for sitting-in at a Woolworth lunch counter in Tallahassee, Florida. A sit-in became the nation's first "Jail-In" when my mother and aunt, along with three other students from Florida A&M University, refused to pay their fine and spent 49 days in jail. To this day, my mother wears dark glasses even indoors after an injury she sustained when a police officer threw a teargas canister in her face during a nonviolent march in 1960.

My father read about my mother's activism in *Jet* magazine and attended law school in Florida to be closer to the civil rights struggle—and he and my mother forged a partnership with civil rights at its core. In 1963, freshly married, they attended the "March on Washington" as special guests, and it seems that they have never rested since. Later, my father represented Dr. King in St. Augustine and spent a career as a community organizer.

Our parents have always been our heroes. They taught us that we could change the world.

Monday, on Martin Luther King Day, my sister and I walked along that same Mall with my father and saw excerpts from a Barack Obama speech on Jumbotrons with other eager attendees. Barack Obama's voice rang from end to end, but we could all hear Dr. King beneath him. In the crowd around us, race had vanished in the wonder-filled eyes and shining faces.

Home. It felt like coming Home.

What a careful line my parents walked as they were raising us—making sure we understood the horrors and hardships of the past, but making certain we never believed that White People were the villains. (We had white godparents who had struggled and suffered in the Movement alongside them, after all.) Teaching us the shortcomings of our nation's practices without losing hope in her ideals. (If they didn't believe, why had they worked so hard?)

My sister and I secured tickets for my parents, but with a wind-chill that made it feel like the teens and streets so blocked that they were a human wall, we made a family decision that they shouldn't face the crowds and the cold…and risk missing the ceremony entirely. Besides,

the tickets we held were in different sections—and the
most important thing, we decided, was to experience the
moment together, as a family.

We experienced the heartache of Miami's 1980 riots as a
family. We experienced my father's late nights as a family.
We experienced NAACP conventions as a family. And we
experienced countless tearful Martin Luther King Day
celebrations as a family, long before the national holiday.
We experienced my parents' emotional wounds as a
family.

We wanted to be within easy reach of each other, within
easy touch.

So, we were. We stood on an eighth-floor perch on the
roof of the Newseum on Pennysylvania Avenue, within
easy walking distance of the Capitol steps on an ordinary
day. From there, we could see the throng of people
gathered at the Mall in the far distance on one end...and
on the other end, dignitaries streamed to their seats where
Barack Hussein Obama was about to be sworn in as the
44th President of the United States.

Barack Hussein Obama? And a family that looks so much
like ours?

It boggles me still.

When the cold became too much for my parents, we
went inside to see and hear more clearly on a large
monitor. Polite police officers clustered on the rooftop
allowed us to pass, and special police with bomb-
sniffing German shepherds patrolled the halls. (Did the
dogs remind my parents of Selma? Of Birmingham? Of
Tallahassee?)

We watched the ceremony, immersed in that wonderful
joy that brings easy tears. "You girls are more emotional
than we are," my mother said, although they shed their
tears too.

I wanted to hear portions of President Obama's inaugural speech outside, so I returned to the rooftop. There, I heard the new president's voice ricocheting up and down Pennsylvania Avenue, to the Mall and back, words colliding with words—but the meaning perfectly clear.

The time had come. The moment had arrived. I felt the mighty cheers from the Mall to my bones. They seemed to rattle the windows and shake the earth.

Later, we stood on the rooftop together when the new president's motorcade returned with its newly inaugurated Commander-in-Chief, passing directly below us with its flashing lights of red and blue. Luckier witnesses on the floor below me actually saw the new president and First Lady unexpectedly climb out of their car to walk and wave while the parade crowds gathered just out of sight screamed with shock and delight.

We will not walk with fear, they said.

A new day. A new generation. A new time.

Maybe now, at last, my parents will feel free to rest their marching feet...and enjoy the world they helped remake.

Tananarive Due is an American Book Award winner and the co-author of Freedom in the Family: A Mother-Daughter Memoir of the Fight for Civil Rights *(with Patricia Stephens Due). Learn more at www. tananarivedue.com.*

A Better History

Victoria Christopher Murray

i was born in the year when a woman who, after a long day of honest work, was escorted off a city bus in Montgomery, Alabama, her wrists bound in handcuffs, because she dared to remain in her seat when a white man told her to stand up so that he could sit down. With that single act, Rosa Parks challenged the deep segregation laws of the South...a society that thrived and survived on legal racism.

Rosa Parks could have been my mother.

I am alive on this day, when a man who proudly wears the name bestowed upon him by his African father, placed his hand on the same Bible that President Lincoln used to take the sacred oath of the highest office in this land. And Barack Obama did this on the steps of the Capitol where slave crews toiled to erect one of the most important symbols of our country.

Barack Obama could have been my brother.

In my lifetime, the walls of separatism, racism and hatred have slowly begun to tumble. This is by no means a post-racial America; it is, however, a progressive America. It is a country that has opened its heart to change.

This will mean so much to my daughter.

Every tear that fell from my eyes as I watched the first African American become president was filled with joy. Every note I sang in the Star Spangled Banner was filled with a renewed love for my country—a love that has always been there, but is enriched now with true feelings of inclusion. And every little black girl and boy I saw filled my heart with expectation—knowing now that when they hear the words, "You can grow up to be whatever you want to be," these children will know those words are true.

I've lived a lifetime of history and now walking into this new time, I want to be better, I want to do better, I want to rise to the call of what's expected. I want to participate in America.

I am so proud to be an American, so proud to live under the political, social, spiritual, emotional tutelage of Barack Obama; the man who has the stature to step into the shoes of change and hope and belief. The man who is truly the President of the United States of the World.

Victoria Christopher Murray is a bestselling novelist whose works include JOY, Truth Be Told, Grown Folks Business, A Sin and a Shame, and The Ex Files. She has received numerous awards, including the Golden Pen Award for Best Inspirational Fiction and the Phyllis Wheatley Trailblazer Award for being the pioneer in African American Christian Fiction. In 2008, she won the African-American Literary Award for Best Novel (Too Little, Too Late). To learn more, visit www.victoriachristophermurray.com.

Those Are My People, Too

Dave Malone

It's almost high noon, and the snow flurries dive beneath a gray winter sky.

I stand in the beige lobby of the Motel 6 in Georgetown, Indiana. It smells like black coffee caking the bottom of a pot.

Big Katie of Hawaii tells me it's okay that I left my keycards in the room. She has good teeth, red cheeks, and I like her wide-mouth bass smile.

I hear TV noise from the far corner. I lean over the bar that separates us and crane my neck to see flashes of red and blue American flags, black, brown and white faces.

The hulking California preacher man, Rick Warren, comes up to the podium. He sports a trimmed goatee and begins the invocation.

I am surprised by the fact of it. I think on separation of church and state. Then, I notice that Big Katie has closed her eyes.

Her right hand rests calmly on the desk, but more important are the three fingers of her left hand, chubby like candy corn, clasped to the desk corner. The prayer goes on. I stare at her, this Buddha of dark clothes and Christian faith. Big Katie's three fingers are locked on that edge. That hand is as rock hard faithful as St. Peter. I have done sitting meditation and I know how difficult it is. Her fingers don't budge while I pick white lint off my black sweater. Finally, Warren finishes.

"That was a very long prayer," I say.

"Not really," she says.

I can't help but like her. Her eyes are deer brown.

"I'll be in the car most of the day. I won't see these clips, " I say…"Thanks for sharing this moment with me."

As I walk down the beige hall, I think about the three-dollar tip I left the smiling maid. And the note: "I wish I could tip you more." I think about the barber in Austin, Texas, who gave out free haircuts at a shelter yesterday. I think about the man from Lexington, Kentucky, who headed a campaign to give out emergency kits to the elderly. Those are my people. And I think about the poets who recited lame poetry on NPR. I even think about the prayers I didn't care for, the patriot speak, and Big Katie's faith. Everyone seemed sincere. So no matter our differences, those are my people, too.

I think about the New Deal that helped my great grandfather pave highways. I wonder if Mr. Obama has the something bold in store for us. But even if he doesn't have that New Deal spirit, it doesn't matter. Ultimately, change has to be inside of each of us.

When I leave the motel, I nod to an African-American man about my age.

"How ya doin'?" he asks me.

"Couldn't be better. How you doin'?"

Georgetown, Indiana is 97% white. But I don't think

either one of us knows that. Neither does Big Katie. After all, it's inauguration day.

Dave Malone has published three books of poetry. He's a vegetarian, soon-to-be marathon runner, film aficionado, and an admitted Francophile.

The Unseen Made Visible

Susan Skolfield

i t is said that in India, people greatly value what cannot be seen. The eyes of those Obama volunteers who had joined me on this journey that culminated on January 20, 2009, demonstrated this value. We were a grassroots office in a small Florida town and we were ready to change the world.

Our eyes expressed a spirit of determination, energy, and light. We were a varied group with faces that were wrinkled and smooth, multi-hued, work-weary, and even a few stress-free. Initially strangers, we bonded with the shared belief that the ship of our union was in peril. Many of us believed she was going down.

Seen every day in the office: a brilliant and kind retired attorney; an efficient ex-hippie with roots in the Deep South; a writer with boundless energy; a Vietnam vet with stories to tell; a shy fifteen-year-old computer whiz, and many more. One by one, we experienced a stirring, a whisper from within: "All hands on deck."

We had families and jobs and responsibilities and concerns yet we found time to give our hearts and energy to the mission. We organized, planned, and rolled up our sleeves. We gave according to our talents, our time, our inclination and our conviction. We were a force. Call by call, door by door, prayer by prayer, even the most skeptical among us began to allow the vision of a better way to enter our souls. We grew in numbers and in confidence.

On the evening of November 4, 2008, our joyful, faces reflected a beautiful synergy of what could not be seen and what could, a confluence of heaven and earth. We discovered that, through individual effort and intention, the ship could be righted. That simple iconic image many of us had not allowed into our minds had materialized.

Now, we were in Washington, D.C., on January 20, 2009, several of us from that little town, joining with nearly two million other freezing Americans to witness and celebrate the course correction of our ship with a brand new leader at the helm. An oath was taken, just 35 words. A cold wind filled the sails and we headed off toward tomorrow, knowing that, when we pull together, our destination is an endless sea of possibility.

Susan Skolfield funded and built a grassroots Obama field office in her hometown of Winter Park, Florida, in 2008. The office attracted tremendous community support and registered 1,400 new voters. With the inauguration over, she looks forward to enjoying many of her pre-campaign activities, including photography, jewelry design and spending time with her siblings and nieces.

Night Fall Sun Rise

Etan Thomas

I never imagined it could happen in my lifetime

As my mind turns back the hands of crimes to a time when
we were rattled in chains

Captured in segregation's pain

But we've climbed our way up the mountainside and
claimed our prize

Our eyes refused to lose focus

Drawing back the shades of history that have eclipsed our
past we've now brightened our future

Now able to ring a bell that once refused to toll for thee

Red white and blue plastered

But we've mastered our own destinies

Reaching heights of dreams deeply rooted in the minds of
kings that withered the storms from sea to shining sea

Nonviolently we're respected by any means

Swimming in endless possibilities

Our arrows of opportunities can hit any targets within the
reach of our mind frame

While the country is filled with elation

It's way past time for a change

Hugs and cheers

Warm embraces from total strangers

Smiles on faces

Cries and tears

Barack Obama's inauguration is a dream come true

He is the anticipated rain of a village suffering through an
eight-year drought

Poorly tended-to roots of a creed that promised freedom
justice and equality for all has become as dry as the
Sahara's sand

The dying crops of morality sound judgment and
respectability have dried like sun-shriveled raisins
throughout the land

Yes we can replenish the fruits of our depleted garden

We're starving for honesty and truth

A new kind of leadership

They tried to extinguish the fire of our passion

Smother our flames with a system that refused to burn
for all

But our dreams would still glow in the dark

Hope for the future has been sparked by an unfamiliar call

Politics as usual no longer holds us hostage

No more running from a bear into the arms of a wolf

Or caught in nets of false promises

This is the dawn of a new day

America's strength could become as solid as a rock

Newfound honor dignity and national pride

Thank God for Barack

Etan Thomas is a poet, peace activist, and center for the NBA's Washington Wizards. He was extremely active in the Obama campaign.

How the Inauguration Affects Me

Margaret Johnson-Hodge

a s the world witnesses the first Black Man to be sworn in as the next President of the United States, I have no choice but to consider the issue of 'Race'. You see, my whole life has been about it. I was born 'Colored,' went on to become a 'Negro,' graduated to being 'Black,' and am now 'African-American'. No other people, in the history of the world, have gone through so many name changes.

'Race' was me, before I was me. My great-great grandmother, Margaret Hinton, was stolen from Africa at the age of twelve and worked on a plantation in North Carolina. My maternal grandmother (the second Margaret) could not marry my maternal grandfather because she was considered too 'dark' to be formally admitted into my grandfather's half Black/half Jewish family.

I was called the 'N' word while living on a Naval Base in Virginia. My white playmate said I was a 'Nigger' and she could no longer play with me. At the time I was five. But even at five, I knew I wasn't 'Nigger'. Too bad she didn't know it too.

My life has been marred with many injustices because of the color of my skin. But on January 20, 2009, as history is

being made, I know from here on in, the world will know
that I not only sing America, I am America too.

*Margaret Johnson-Hodge is the author of nine novels,
including* The Real Deal, Butterscotch Blues, True Lies,
and Some Sunday. *Her most recent*, Red Light, Green
Light, *was published in 2008. She has received numerous
awards and her books regularly find themselves on the
bestseller lists of* Essence and Black Expression. *To learn
more, visit www.mjhodge.net.*

Something to Talk About

Anna van Slee

every day—countless times each day—I start writing an e-mail..."Hi so-and-so! How are you?" ...and I pause.

Seated in front of my computer at work, I take sip of piping-hot coffee and search for a sentiment. Some piece of humanity I can inject into a business communication. That one filler sentence that will help build a connection; place a buffer between my greeting and the real reason I'm typing. It can't be too personal, or long-winded. (The weather's a dependable stand-by. Something everyone can relate to. Brief. Safe.)

It's usually an uncomfortable, frustrating moment. But not the day of the inauguration. I could forge onward and type: "Any plans for watching the inauguration?" I could silently warm my fingers against the ceramic of my mug and open the conference call with: "Are you all taking a break later to watch the ceremony?"

The responses were interesting, but anti-climactic. One company opened its cafeteria and served everyone cake while they watched the events unfold on a big-screen TV. Another handed out Obama t-shirts, and let people take a one-hour break to watch on their computers.

I was disappointed. Without realizing it, I had expected
more than bland platitudes. I wanted to hear excitement,
relief, anger--anything. In the end, it was just another bland
holiday. Emotion safely avoided.

On my way home from work, I stopped at the bank. I
had to go in to talk to the teller rather than use the ATM
because I only had $10 left in my account.

I haven't filled out a withdrawal slip in years. While
the girl looked up my account number for me, an
uncomfortable silence settled in and almost without
thinking I asked, "Did you watch the inauguration this
morning?"

The girl looked up at me, her face a mask of mock horror:
"No!" she screeched. "Can you believe it?! I mean, such
an historic event. And I had to watch replays on my lunch
hour. And...I supported Obama. I went down to Grant Park.
Did you go? It was amazing..."

She was outraged and overjoyed and brimming over
with all the words I'd been waiting to hear all day. It was
like I had uncorked a champagne bottle of emotion.

I had so desperately wanted the day not to be Just
Another Day. And in the end, it wasn't.

*Anna van Slee is a project manager living in Chicago with
her wizard husband Pato and two little furry old men,
Mr. Francis and Mr. Obie. When she laughs, her eyes
water—a trait she inherited from her grandpa, Frank
Gorski, to whom she dedicates this piece.*

Inauguration Day

Malinda Williams

On Tuesday, January 20, 2009, at 12:00 noon, Barack Obama will become the 44th President of the United States. At about the same time two years ago, this dynamic, charismatic man was campaigning his way around the United States, determined to win the Democratic nomination for the 2008 presidential election. I, living what I thought was a pretty good life in a very liberal and open-minded society, was struggling with how I was going to vote from an unbiased and politically well-informed place.

Though I can't honestly say that my decision was made in the way I had hoped, my struggle came to an end almost instantly when a woman approached me in a department store and commented on how handsome and well-behaved my son was. Always the proud mother, I gushed "Thank you". She then placed her hand on my son's head, looked him in the eyes and asked, "When you grow up, do you want to be a basketball player, or a singer?" A bit furious, a bit shocked and a bit hurt, I grabbed my son's hand and proceeded to leave the store, but not before I barked "he will more likely be a brain surgeon or a scientist."

I decided that day, that I would vote for Barack Obama and I never looked back. To the contrary, I've only looked forward. I've looked forward to Inauguration Day. The day that would not only symbolize, but also solidify that the "dream" would no longer be deferred and my son could then add "world leader" to his list of future aspirations.

Malinda Williams has starred in several movies, including, High School High, The Wood, First Sunday and Idlewild. Her next feature, Nailed, will be released in 2009. She stars in the hit series Soul Food on Showtime. In 2003 and 2004, Malinda was nominated for NAACP Image Awards for Outstanding Actress in a Drama Series for Soul Food.

Pass the Lemon Butter Sauce Dear, the Obamas Are Here

James A. Almond

Living just four miles from the White House, you might think that the decision to attend the Obama Inauguration would be an easy one. Trouble is, we live on the Arlington side of the Potomac, and getting across the iceberg-filled river over bridges would require a very early morning walk at 15 degrees for a five or six-hour stand with two million people sharing portolets.

Sure, we could take the Metro or a bus, but there again is the issue of personal discomfort in frigid conditions. That was the argument that I presented my very enthusiastic and eager-to-attend wife. Don't get me wrong, we are strong Obama supporters, worked the polls and such. We even have an official invitation, yet I contemplated, "From where we'll probably stand the only people we will see are the people standing next to us, and if we are lucky, maybe we'll catch a glimpse of a jumbotron."

That still did not dissuade her.

So then, I thought of something else. "How about I get a couple of lobsters and a bottle of champagne and I put a fire in the fireplace and we turn on MSNBC for full coverage?"

Thank heaven that was convincing enough.

Now, we could see the whole event, with all the emotion and loving enthusiasm from millions of people. We could see their tears and hear their constant cheers. We could see Obama, Michelle, and those absolutely precious little girls, and the temperature is 72 degrees.

Pass the lemon butter sauce dear, the Obamas are here.

James A. George is a writer originally from north central Ohio who now resides in Arlington, Virginia. He is also a watercolorist who produces quick sketches in people settings. He writes technical books and wants WEBook to be his venue for creative works.

A Sigh of Relief...

Rebecca Jackson

On November 4th I was sitting in a fast food restaurant in St. Petersburg, Florida, watching the results of the votes come in via MSNBC. I was amongst a number of campaign volunteers who were alive with anticipation in spite of weeks of negligible sleep. Sitting beside me was my then fiance who worked on the campaign in several states throughout 2008. I had been an 'Obama widow' for much of the year, going up to five weeks at a time without seeing him. It had been emotionally tough and quite lonely at times; however, I knew it was all in aid of something potentially incredible.

I've never felt so passionate about an election in my entire life until 2008. I'm not a U.S. citizen so I couldn't even vote, yet that seemed immaterial. I was fully invested owing to my fiance's deep involvement but also my own personal belief in Obama's candidacy. Besides, the entire world was captivated by this race, desperately hoping for an Obama win. This was an election like no other.

During the course of the year, I had wondered many times if I could comfortably continue to live in the U.S. if McCain actually won. The McCain/Palin ticket seemed totally incongruent with my own values and those of most people I cared about, both inside the U.S. and outside. There was a lot at stake that night on a personal, national and international level. Oh, and I haven't even mentioned that we were due to get married in two days time! For most of the year Obama had been the third person in our relationship--I had shared my fiance with the campaign and often found myself in second place. So, I had an understandably selfish desire for an Obama win just to ensure my fiance would be in high spirits on our wedding day.

As the results trickled in the energy in the bar sizzled. The juxtaposition of our table with its excitement and fervor and the table behind which comprised four people whose faces could not be more grim underlined the deep partisan rifts central to this election. The more jovial we became as more states were won, the more morose they appeared until they abruptly left. Several times during the evening I interrupted my rising enthusiasm to wonder what, if any, backlash might occur if Obama made it.

And then suddenly and unexpectedly everything was over. Obama's victory was declared relatively early in the proceedings and we were somewhat taken aback. There were tears, laughter and much imbibing of alcohol in the aftermath. I felt an immense amount of pride watching Obama's acceptance speech. My bond with my adopted home deepened markedly that night while the rest of the world breathed a huge sigh of relief.

Rebecca Jackson grew up in Birmingham, England and now lives in Brooklyn, New York. She has a particular affinity for mimicking pterodactyls, which is how she first won over her husband. Her other interests include neuroplasticity, horse-riding, scrabble, and eating.

In an African Village

Leah Noyes

e lection Day

In a small African village, Osia, a local elder, followed the U.S. elections on his black and white television. He was accompanied by his neighbour Amino, his wife and their half-naked children. Their eyes were glued to the small screen sitting on a slanting table. Each time Barack Obama's photo flashed before them, they erupted in excitement. Although the loud generator outside made it difficult to follow the news, they knew the results when they saw celebrations in the American crowd, and the many displays of Obama photos. When Obama walked onto to the platform amidst jubilation to give the historical speech, Osia did not understand a word; however he was excited by the tone of his voice.

Judging by the reaction of the crowd; tears running down their cheeks, jumping up and down and hugging each other, Osia knew Obama was a special man. A man capable of holding the attention of big crowds. He too felt his impact although he couldn't explain it; he wiped a tear using the tip of his shirt, Amino also wiped a tear with his handkerchief. "How could a man so far feel so near?" Amino asked. "How is he relevant to us?" he added. Osia couldn't answer. He looked outside to catch a glimpse of the sun that had started to set. "I know the sun will be shining in our lives for a long time", he muttered.

Inauguration Day

On Inauguration day Osia watched the ceremony with a bigger crowd outside the village pub. The fairly big screen that was raised outside attracted the whole village. Women with babies strapped on their backs giggled as they joined their husbands in the celebrations. Some of the youth climbed up trees to have a better view. Others opted to sit inside the bar, a mud-thatched hut with an open roof. The small room was full beyond its capacity; it looked like it could burst. A strong smell of millet beer filled the air.

Voices were raised in excitement when Obama put his hand on the bible used by former President Abraham Lincoln to take the oath. When he mentioned the small African village where his father was born, the cheers were deafening. Everyone joined in the traditional dance as their clothes soaked in sweat. "It is like a dream, I have never felt so much hope and freedom since independence," said one of the elders as he sucked hard on the local brew.

"Obama is our son. I feel as though he is my president," said Osia.

Leah Noyes, a Ugandan, formerly worked as a journalist for the Daily Monitor *in Uganda. She now lives in the UK, where she works in the communication department for an international charity.*

The Obama Brotherhood

Meagen Farrell

my son learned to clap just in time for the Inauguration. He's eight months old. Like the other infants in our play group, he showed no interest as the parents watched the ceremony. But he looked at me when the adults all cheered after Barack Obama concluded, "…so help me God." I smiled and clapped. After a pause, a grin spread across his face, displaying his four baby teeth and dimples. He laughed and clapped in return.

We create the world for our children, then they absorb it and make it their own. On November 4th, the American people voted not just to change policies, but to affect the subconscious of our newest generation. A three-year-old boy we know learned the alphabet this year, and every time he sees O, he says, "Obama!"

What will this name mean to our children? Right now, the message says: By working hard, any person, of any heritage, from any neighborhood in this country can achieve his dreams. Even in our neighborhood, Hough, even in our city, Cleveland, Foreclosure Capitol. But I worry about the residual obstacles, buried like landmines in our society and institutions. There is still so much work to be done. During his Whistle-Stop Tour riding the train to the White House, Obama warned, "Now it falls to us to ensure that everyone in this country can make it if they try."

For some, hopelessness was the only thing standing in their way. Now that it has been replaced by inspiration, nothing will stop them. The past couple months has brought an influx of young black men coming to register for my GED classes. I once considered them an unreachable demographic, their skills ignored by our sit-still-and-test-well system of education. But every week, more arrive in twos and threes, bringing friends and brothers. Most are not only registering; they are staying, studying, doing homework, passing tests. I call them "The Obama Brotherhood," and they are reaching towards the light of opportunity that has begun to break through.

I say a prayer for my students, and for our children. I imagine these street-hardy young men watching Barack Obama take the oath of office. Are they looking at their children clapping? Are their children playing "Politics," practicing their inaugural speeches? I look at my son, shaking a rattle, wondering what names he will see on his first ballot. What kind of world will our children create together?

Meagen Farrell is a full-time mother and part-time adult educator, educational consultant, writer, and trainer for Farrell Ink. Before they became parents, she and her husband (and a lot of friends and family!) rehabilitated an old abandoned home in Cleveland, Ohio.

Can We Get a Witness?

Lionel Beasley

in 2006, Barack Obama came to the University of Vermont to give a speech at the Ira Allen Chapel in support of the congressional campaign of Peter Welch, whose predecessor, Bernie Sanders, was making his own run at a Senate seat. Jeffrey, a politically aware friend, suggested going, and we agreed to meet in line an hour beforehand. Thinking back on the day, it's hard to resist the temptation to recall the moment through an ironic construction of hindsight destiny, a sense that the '08 presidential election result was somehow inevitable, the natural outcome of eight painful years under the Bush/Cheney junta and a sea-change brought by the great flow of history.

From my office window on that late winter day, I could see the line build fully three hours before the speech. By the time I met Jeffrey, the line snaked through snow and ice past several campus buildings. In line, the crowd was wired as if waiting for a concert or a big game; ultimately, it proved far too large for the 500-seat chapel, forcing the vast majority into overflow seating in the CC Theater. Which is where I saw him, on a big overhead screen in a full auditorium, piped in by a closed-circuit system operated with great difficulty by people who looked suspiciously like members of a campus A/V club.

What we saw then was not simply the Barack Obama of the '04 Democratic convention—that wonky practicality paired with soaring rhetoric. It was something entirely new, a transcendent vision of politics as it could be if only we made better, smarter choices. When he was done, I turned to Jeffrey and said, "That man is going to be the first black president someday." Silently, I added a quick calculation: 2012 perhaps, or more likely, 2016. As much as I might now claim some status as a new-age, socio-political Nostradamus, there was no way then that I suspected I'd be watching the events of today, a mere two years later. On the way out of the CC Theater I felt compelled to shake my head and add, "Too bad his middle name is Hussein."

Up until that moment, I had simply accepted as a given that no African-American would be president in my lifetime. And why shouldn't I have? Despite the electricity of the overwhelmingly white crowd at UVM, I could only see it through the lens of my time and incidents scarred in memory. I can remember a moment from my childhood in the early 70's, a St. Patrick's Day spent out and about with my mother. I'd been nagging her that I had to pee; we stopped in an Irish bar. When my mother asked after the facilities, the bartender responded, "Nigger, go back to Harlem." I can remember watching busing riots on television, and I saw, even with a child's understanding, the effect all around me of the white flight that followed integration. I remember being told in the 80's that I wasn't black, or was, at the very least, 'not like others,' for failing to match stereotypes provided by films and television.

In the late 80's, I got mad when the Rodney King verdict came down, I blasted "F*** tha Police" on my stereo for several hours, before heading out to look for the riot, for cop cars to burn and overturn. I ground my teeth with every atrocity committed by NY Police Department. I can remember slipping *Bizarre Ride II the Pharcyde* into the CD player and grooving to "If I Were President," as the crazy fantasy of any young, black male born to a certain time and place.

Then, in the 00's, just as I thought America might truly be shifting toward a more colorblind society, Hurricane Katrina happened; what followed, of course, was a terrible spectacle of death and suffering, repackaged for mass consumption as a Michael Bay remake of Birth of a Nation, a clear illustration of the inevitability of black male mayhem—of looting, rape, arson and murder. It seemed all too easy for the vast majority to believe any wild rumor out of New Orleans, revealing lingering white fears and anxieties that seemed surprisingly resilient, and stubbornly implacable.

And so, here we are; it would be easy to lend too much significance to the fact of the first black president, as if hundreds of years of ugly history could be tidied up with a particularly good day. But the reality of the result and the celebrations that have followed cannot be denied. I watched the election returns with Jeffrey and his wife Sherry, and when the race was called, we popped a bottle of champagne and toasted. All night, we'd talked of that speech at the chapel in '06 and recalled our initial assessments of his chances at the presidency; since that day and his subsequent announcement, I'd only thought of him as the best candidate, with race as a secondary factor at best. It was only when the election was called that the magnitude of the event struck me: A black man is going to be the President of the United States of America. He was the best candidate and he won. Of course; it seems simple if you ignore the entire length and breadth of American history

Hearing the roar of a crowd coming up Main Street on election day, we went out into it. Later, we found out that same thing had happened spontaneously all over America, people celebrating their vote and the fact that so many others had made the same choice. At long last, the better, smarter choice. And I wondered what my grandmother would have made of this, born an orphan into a Jim Crow world near the turn of the century and raised by her own grandmother, an ex-slave. She was born two months after the Titanic sank, but lived to see men walk on the moon and the millennium, wonders beyond her youthful comprehension. She died in 2000 at 87, having lived a full life. But I wish now that she'd had 8 more years to live to see this, the world cheering the ascension of an African-American family. I can't help wondering what she and so many others—heroes of the Civil Rights Struggle, plain folks ground down by bigotry and hate, or people like my grandmother who thrived in spite of it—would have thought of 01/20/09.

Lionel Beasley is a graduate student at the University of Vermont pursuing a Masters in English. He was born and raised in New York City and has lived in Burlington, Vermont since 2002.

in-auguration

Kevin Walsh

   at noon on the twentieth of january as our forty-forth president was taking oath for office, i sat on my porch in the icy winter cold and scribbled a poem onto a piece of notebook paper till the ink froze up in my pen. that poem is as follows....

The black man walks
  into a white house.
  Tentatively
  at first,
  as all the shades have been
  drawn inside.
  Walking from room to room
  he stops
  to open curtains
  raise the blinds
  and unlatch the shutters.
  He wonders how long

since the sunlight
  shined in these rooms.
  A faded cowboy hat hangs from a rusty nail
  in a room that smells of mold and mildew.
  He lifts the hat;

below it crudely sketched in pencil
 is a child-like drawing of two
 buildings
 both on fire.
 He hangs the hat back on its nail
 and removes a pen

from his breast pocket.
 Below the drawing he writes,

fear.

Above the hat, in large letters,

hope.

He turns to the window and opens it, hoping
 to remove the stale smell from the room.

On the front lawn new neighbors are gathered.

They wave and smile;

as he smiles and waves back

he thinks to himself
 I'm home

Kevin Walsh was born with a pen in one hand and a writing tablet in another, which made it quite difficult for his mother to birth him. She still sports a caesarian scar from the base of her neck to her right knee. It was a large pen.

A Soldier Not Forgotten

Kaitlyn Krone

my uncle is a colonel in the U.S. Army. He has been to some of the most exotic places in the world. He can pretty much choose where he gets stationed. That is why I was surprised when I found out he volunteered to go to Iraq again. I have family and friends in Iraq and Afghanistan constantly, like many other families. And like other families, I am anxious until they are safely back home.

Last year, our worst nightmare became reality not once, but twice. Troops were moving to another location and some hidden enemies threw a bomb onto the hood of my uncle's truck. Luckily it was a dud.

The next time he was not so lucky. He was going to get his mail like he did any other day when there was an air raid. We received a copy of the commander's report of the attack. It was like reading an excerpt out of a war novel. The account was so detailed. A bomb had landed not too far from my uncle. He was thrown into a nearby jeep, which had been demolished as well. His legs were pinned in twisted metal and he had lost a lot of blood by the time they found him. He ended up with a chunk of muscle missing from his calf. Doctors weren't sure if he was going to be able to keep his leg.

Shortly after the attack, he was flown to a hospital in Washington, D.C. The doctors there attempted a procedure to try and replace some of the missing muscle. They told him not to give up hope. Luckily he recovered and has regained some use of his leg.

The whole point of this horror story is this: he received an invitation to the inauguration ceremony. He had just had another surgery and was unable to attend. He was extremely disappointed. Last weekend something happened that made up for that. My uncle was visited by Barack Obama himself.

It was the weekend before Obama was to become our president. Surely he had a schedule full of things to attend to. Yet he took the time to visit with my uncle. He even took pictures with him. I was beside myself.

Obama is a good, caring person. I made sure I watched the inauguration and cheered him on. I had my apprehensions about him, but all of that was pushed out of my mind as I watched him take that oath. I had pride for my country in my heart and tears in my eyes.

Kaitlyn Krone, 19, is attending college in Buffalo, New York, where she has lived her entire life. She has been writing stories, poetry, and essays since she was six.

Spider-Man, Giant Heads of Easter Island, and Macaroni and Cheese

Larry King

i t was a historic day. A time to celebrate. An occasion to break out the party hats, cheese curls, and frozen pizza.

No, I'm not talking about the premier of the new season of Lost. I'm speaking of the inauguration of our 44th President of the United States of America, Barack Obama.

I'm very excited. Not only because he's a dynamic personality who will bring intelligence and compassion to the White House for a change. And not only because he will lead this great nation to new heights after years of losing its direction. But there is something about him that appeals to the people everywhere.

Most people focus on Obama's differences: the fact he's an African-American with a foreign-sounding name. But I find myself identifying with him more than any other president. He's my age, he grew up in humble beginnings, and he read Spider-Man comic books as a kid. How cool is that?

It's still hard to believe we elected a black man to the highest office in the land. I think I would have been less surprised if we chose one of the giant stone heads of Easter Island as president.

So, on the morning of his inauguration, I did what any red-blooded, patriotic American would do. I called in sick so I could stay home and watch it on television.

My supervisor was suspicious when I told him I couldn't make it in. "Are you really sick? Or are you just staying home to watch the inauguration?" he asked.

"No," I said. "I'm really sick. I have...er....head lice. Yeah, that's it. Head lice."

"Really? Is it bad?"

"Absolutely. It's this super-mutated strain that's infested the whole house. In fact, I've been quarantined in my own home. I've got people in containment suits from the Centers for Disease Control, and they're spraying the whole place down. It's a mess here. I may be gone awhile."

"Did you get it out of your hair?"

"Who said it was in my hair?"

He paused as if contemplating whether to ask for details. He wisely dropped the subject. "Okay, just get back to work as soon as possible."

So I spent the rest of the day watching coverage of Obama's journey through this momentous day. I saw the speech. Then I saw analysis of the speech. And then I saw analysis of the analysis of the speech. I also witnessed Barack and Michelle shaking their money-makers at various balls. And I saw George W. Bush riding off into

the sunset in his helicopter, leaving behind a legacy of
wars, torture, financial disasters, complete disregard
of the Constitution and general buffoonery. Mission
accomplished!!

At about 5 p.m., my 18-year-old son Cory called in a
panic. "It's been five hours, and there's been no change.
Where's the change? I expected rocket jet packs and robot
maids. But I still have to walk three blocks to the grocery
store to buy my macaroni and cheese, and I had to cook it
myself."

Now, this may seem to be a severe overreaction to the
situation, but in Cory's defense, he really loves macaroni
and cheese.

"Calm down, son," I said in my best Mr. Brady
impersonation (Note: That would be Mike Brady, patriarch
of the television family "The Brady Bunch", not NFL
quarterback Tom Brady. I avoid using my Tom Brady voice
because I'm usually sacked by a 280-pound linebacker
from out of nowhere. Very disconcerting.)

Anyway, I added a comforting, "After all, Rome wasn't
built in a day."

"They didn't have rocket jet packs or robot maids either,"
Cory said. "And look what happened. It burned to the
ground."

I didn't quite know how I answer this comment, so I put
Cory on hold and went back to the television.

In summary, it was a great day. Barack Obama delivered
a message of hope. Hope for a future built on brotherhood
and tolerance. Someday, we'll look past our prejudices
and differences and learn to accept everybody, regardless
of their race, religion, gender or sexual orientation.
Someday we'll all embrace each other and live together in
peace and love.

Who knows, maybe our next president will be a woman. Or maybe an openly gay person. Or maybe, just maybe, our next President will be one of those stone heads of Easter Island. You just never know.

Larry King is a postal worker from Missoula, Montana who enjoys eating waffles for breakfast.

A Volunteer in VA

Sue Heilbronner

i volunteered all day of the general election in the largest precinct in Loudoun County, Virginia. The precinct was about 45 minutes from my home in Maryland, but many regarded Loudoun as a "swing county" in a swing state, and I wanted to have the kind of impact I couldn't have in my dark blue town. Loudoun is a DC suburb that has grown tremendously in the last four years, making it more diverse, less rural, and, in theory, more likely to be meaningful to Barack Obama.

I spent that day at a local high school, "womaning" a table that was the legal minimum number of feet from the front door of the polling station. I wore layers of long underwear, sweaters, and a colorful Obama t-shirt over the ensemble. The Obama volunteers were outnumbered by the McCain volunteers by three to one most of the day, but I was pumped.

When we arrived at 6 a.m. in pitch darkness, it felt like the Super Bowl. Cars were streaming in, and 400 people waited in line in the brutal cold for the polls to open at 7. We handed out what we called "Democratic Sample Ballots." The Republican volunteers handed out what they called "Sample Ballots." We were already off to a fiery start.

There were two great moments that day (or three, if you count the moment CNN announced for Obama later that night). Over the course of the day, I grew confident in my ability to "pick" party affiliation by the clues one might look for if one were, hypothetically, standing in front of a polling place for 13 hours offering occasional help and trying to be upbeat ("Thanks for voting!" "Want a post-vote lollipop for the kids?"). Virginia forbade campaign clothing inside the polls, so it was pure guesswork for anyone who didn't curse at me or give me a hug.

Sure, race seemed like a good indicator. The precinct was amazingly diverse, and it seemed pretty clear that almost every "person of color" was thrilled to be there to pull the lever for Obama. Of course there were also plenty of white folks like me who supported Barack. But my informal Caucasian profiling led me to believe that the people who drove up in super-sized SUVs, wore Brooks Brothers suits and shiny shoes, and used mousse in their hair probably were not in our camp. I couldn't even get a "good morning" out of them. I got more than a few sneers.

Then this 20-something guy walked up. He looked like a nice-suit-shiny-shoe-polo-player who was taking the day off. Timberland sweatshirt, square jaw. He walked briskly by me on his way inside. No Democratic Sample Ballot for him. On his way out, I mumbled, "Thanks for voting." He spun around, lifted up his sweatshirt and proudly puffed out his Obama Hope t-shirt. "I worked this precinct during the primaries," he gushed. "What a great day!"

A few hours later, a model-worthy, light-skinned black woman dressed in a professional pencil-skirt suit approached. It was apparent from her gait and fixed face that she did not suffer fools. As such, she paid me no mind. While she voted, I wondered whether this take-no-prisoners gal was in there choosing Sarah Palin. I caught her as she strode back by me on her way to the parking lot. "Thanks for voting?" I muttered. Five steps past me, as I recovered from the sheer onslaught of her steely confidence, she threw up her hands in victory, shook her bod a bit and danced her way to her car.

That dance was surely for me. And that is when I knew to a certainty that we as a country–as close to racially unified as we had ever been–were going to be brave, step up, and change everything.

Sue Heilbronner toils on weekdays at WEbook and on weekends on the links. She hails from Miami but lives in DC, which she believes will at last be a cool place to live for a change.

Looking In, Hopeful

MJ Heiser

Last night I dreamed that my whole family—uncles, sisters, brothers, nieces, nephews, cousins, everyone—attended the Inauguration. The venue, a nondescript but gigantic theater hall, found it necessary to convert some of the concession areas to accommodate the crowd. We were seated in one of these concession conversions. We had been allowed to come, but we were still separate.

I remember walking away from my family in the dream. I remember not being able to feel their overwhelming joy and anticipation, not being swept up, like they were, in the manic frenzy of the moment. They were arrayed in the red, white, and blue of the moment. I was in my traditional costume of brown.

I stepped out to the service areas, where the Secret Service men stood guard and the venue employees hustled to maintain the illusion that it was easy, effortless, and predestined. I watched them, their faces drawn and tense. None of them wanted to ruin Obama's big day. I understood completely.

I wasn't looking for meaning in this dream when I woke, but I found plenty once I gave myself the space and time to reflect. I am not a Republican. I am not a Democrat. I am not white, or black, or Asian, or Native American. I am not straight or gay. I am a woman who straddles many lines of definition in this culture of polar opposites. I don't pick a side when I'm asked to do so.

I did not vote for Barack Obama. I did not vote for John McCain. I voted, but in order to fulfill the dictates of my conscience, I had to write in my candidate, who of course did not even register in the results. To keep the promise I made when I gave up my Filipino dual citizenship to focus on being an American—the promise to vote not with my heart, but with my head—I can not belong to either of the two parties in power.

Because I do not belong to any one party, race, religion, or sexual orientation, I am often ostracized, viewed with suspicion, or pitied. It's not as bad as it reads here, but in the context of the dream I had last night, I understand it perhaps a little better. Space is made for us at the table, but it's far away from the action, from the spotlight, from the laughter. We are included, but as an afterthought.

However, I am hopeful. I have hope that our new president, a man who is also from a mixed heritage, can give a new, popular face to this issue. I hope his multicultural background makes it easier for people to see everyone who is not one thing or another, but many things.

Even as one who is looking in from the outside, I have hope.

MJ Heiser lives in Austin, Texas. By day, she's a claims examiner for a small professional liability insurance carrier. By night, she's an aspiring novelist and the supportive wife of a talented bassist who also, unfortunately, has a day job.

White Boy

John Meils

It was a month before Obama announced his candidacy. I was at a dinner party thrown by a friend who'd gone to Harvard Law a few years after Barack. Aside from me, almost everyone at the table was like the host—outspoken, black, Ivy-League educated. We were already through drinks and most of dinner and no one had said a word about Obama. I didn't understand. A black man was about to enter the most important election of our lives and nobody seemed interested in talking about it.

"So," I said, pouncing on a break in conversation, "what do you guys think? Can he win?"

Everyone went silent, as all eyes turned my way.

"No," someone said finally. "Not a chance," added another guy.

I was floored. I'd recently come out of a long relationship with a black woman. I knew how some people looked at me and my ex when we walked down the street, how our families felt when they learned we were together, how it forever altered my perspective on race. Still, I thought Obama had a puncher's chance. At the very least, I figured everyone at that table wanted to feel the same.

"This country will never elect a black man," said someone else, ending the conversation.

Leave it to the white boy, I thought. Instead of starting a hopeful debate, I'd reminded everyone at the table that a new chapter in a history of disappointment could soon be written. Worse, I reinforced my own beliefs about the pitfalls of talking race in mixed company. I'd embarrassed myself, my friend, and everyone else in the room.

When Barack was on the precipice of victory, I spoke on the phone with my friend.

"Okay," I said, treading carefully. "He's gonna win. Now do you believe?"

"Almost," he said, "but keep in mind that they take things away from black people in this country right when we want them most."

"C'mon," I pleaded, wondering why my usually positive friend had chosen that moment to be cynical.

After I hung up the phone, I thought about what he said and realized just how much Obama had risked running for president. I also understood why he pounded the idea of hope so hard during the campaign. Because without it, none of us—regardless of skin color—would have the courage to move beyond our old beliefs. For that alone, this white boy is thankful he won.

John Meils is an editor at WEbook. He waited until after Barack Obama was elected to take the job just so he wouldn't miss anything on CNN.

Next Year, Around Now

Patrick van Slee

J oyce the bartender was throwing an inauguration party at our local dive bar. The place was a dump, we liked to say, Yeah. But it was our dump. No better way to usher in the new era of progressive policymaking than with cockroaches and $2.50 PBRs. Cheers to the new era.

For a city that gave the country its new president, the atmosphere in Chicago that day was surprisingly subdued. I don't know exactly what I expected. Something like New Year's Eve, maybe, seasoned a little bit with some excited political chatter. People drunk in the streets? A mirror of the Washington fervor flickering on the boxy television sets hanging over the bar, where crowds charged with positive energy gazed lovingly at their new president? I didn't detect any additional positivity on my way to the bar.

My wife, Anna, and I joined a few of our friends at a table near the window. It was toasty inside, and we shed our coats and draped them over the barstools as we said our hellos. The turnout to the party was low. A few pockets of folks talking quietly, and Joyce handing out apple cider and peanut butter cookies. Every so often someone would glance at one of the TVs and make an awed comment. "All those people," someone would say. "I can't believe it. You'd think this guy was Jesus handing out gobs of free money."

"Everyone blew their wad back in November," said Dave. He gulped at his whiskey. Once the beloved bouncer here, tonight he satisfied himself with being its beloved drunk. "Who gives a crap about all this pomp and ceremony, anyway. The best part for me was watching Bush finally leave on that damn helicopter."

I tipped my beer toward Dave and sent him a nod. "I don't know about you," I said, "but once he got into that thing it seemed like it took a million years for it to lift off."

Laughter. "Yeah," said Anna, "I was watching Obama watch it rev up from the steps of the capitol building. You could tell he was totally thinking, 'Man, will you just get the hell out of here already?'"

More laughs. Matt and Dave's wife Katie got up to get some shots. I glanced at the TV again. There was the helicopter we were just talking about, replayed again, fading off into the hazy winter sky. Adios and goodbye.

That was it, really. Today wasn't the big day. Better to fast-forward to a year from today. Since November, we'd all been impatient for that perspective which would allow us to see the past eight years of traumatizing absurdity from the outside in. Of the six of us sitting there, all with college degrees, half were unemployed. Hundreds of thousands of Americans, Iraqis and others were now dead that didn't need to be. While we looked forward to being pleased with our government, we were so used to despising it that it was almost difficult to imagine life any other way. All that was left was to wait for clues that the world and our lives were getting better.

The door swung open and more folks arrived on the chilly draft, but the bar didn't seem any fuller. Someone put *Here Comes Your Man* on the jukey, and Anna and I started bobbing our heads in unison. Dave fell off his bar stool and lay on the floor, yelling at the filthy ceiling. "I'm that guy! I just became that guy!" Behind the bar Joyce slammed some empties into the trash and told him he was cut off, but then she brought us some more cookies. It was maybe eleven-thirty.

Patrick van Slee lives in Chicago. He has two fat cats and a wife who can triple-flip aerial roundhouse kick his hair into a more pleasing shape. He wishes he were President of the United States of America, but he thinks Barack Obama is probably a better choice.

Aretha's Hat

Hope Henry

It is important that each of us has our own fashion even in the dead of winter or the heat of summer. It can be a different color of hair. It can be earrings that are not in the ears. Fashion can appear in the clothes we wear or the shoes we choose. Better still, on a chilly Tuesday in January during Obama's inauguration, fashion can arrive in the type of hat chosen to wear for the occasion.

Many of the newscasters who reported during the inauguration were wearing mufflers over their ears, berets and fur trapper caps. Spectators watching Obama take his oath wore a rainbow of colors in the form of woolen caps with slogans of "Yes We Can" plastered on the front. Senator Teddy Kennedy came to the event in a fedora. My daughter showed up to the Mall in Washington D.C., wearing a black fake fur helmet, which covered her head and her ears at the same time.

But the creme de la creme of hats appeared on the head of the world-famous singer, Aretha Franklin, fondly called "The Queen of Soul." Aretha arrived on stage during the inauguration extravaganza—during which she gave a rousing performance of Samuel Smith's "My Country Tis of Thee"—topped with a large grey, crystal-studded bow, lined with small Swarovski crystals around the edges. The showpiece seemed almost too large for her face. Her hat has been photographed, filmed and recorded over the

airwaves, across the wires, and around the globe. Aretha's headgear surely will ignite the fashion world and render hats the rage!

As we begin this new presidency with words of "Change" and "Hope," it is pleasing to know that even our fashion can affect change. A highlight of the inauguration ceremony on that cold January afternoon with the blue, cloudless sky will be Aretha's hat.

Hope Henry teaches boys in a detention center in Maryland. She has lived on four continents and had her work published in magazines, newspapers, and wire services. She has also written a children's book and worked as a radio announcer, TV news editor, and photographer.

Mr. Scott

Lisa Ann Flint

dear Mr. Scott:

Had you just lived a little longer you would have seen this most historic event. One that you never, ever thought you would see, but you had Faith that it would happen.

All day I have thought about you and how amazing a man you were and would have been in front of the TV or fighting to get a ticket to the Inauguration itself. You would have gathered all your children and grandchildren around the TV and made them witness this very moment in time, not just for them, but for you to experience it with them.

You taught me to see beyond color and you taught me to look into the eyes of another Human Being.

Your eyes would have been glistening from the tears of joy and expectations, and you would have been honking that nose of yours and saying, "there ain't no shame in a man cryin!"

We all miss you so very much. The house you kept so warm and full of food and love is sold off, but you taught us that it's the soul that keeps those memories alive and that it is our place to instill that in our future generations.

Our new president gives me hope. He inspires me to remember all that you taught me and for me to teach others. Our president will be a teacher to many of us, just like you were to so many.

So with this Mr. Scott, or Paw Paw, as the kids all called you, stand on your cloud in Heaven and look down on this day. Know that so many have the hope.

But it's the Faith, and the soul of a Human Being, that will make this work.

Lisa Ann Flint lives in Louisiana. She is the mother of two, the "meemaw" of one, and the Godmom of a very eccentric eight-year old. She is dedicating her essay to her daughters Kelci and Halei.

Yes We Did

Alison J. Walkley

the first election I voted in was the Kerry v. Bush race when I was 19. I remember the excitement I felt when I walked toward the voting booth the day I became an active American citizen. I remember sitting with a room full of Democrats watching the numbers roll in.

I also remember the disappointment I felt when Kerry lost in an upset.

Four years later, however, I no longer feel cheated by that race. Now I realize why the past eight years have unfolded as they have–to prepare the national landscape for a young senator from Illinois to rise as our political messiah.

Barack Obama was never the perfect presidential candidate for a variety of reasons. He lacks the experience an older contender brings to the table; he has a young family that requires his attention; and, most obviously, he is part African-American, a trait that would have spelled doom before now.

Before this past election, I had lost faith in my fellow Americans. I sensed an overwhelming apathy across the nation for everything happening in the world. Instead of caring about the international HIV/AIDS pandemic, the majority turned a blind eye. It is a lot easier to put stock into the relationships of Hollywood celebrities than to acknowledge the war in the Middle East. The worse shape the world is in, the more Americans flee to their bubbles where they concern themselves with beauty and dieting, rather than life-and-death situations that are reality for the rest of the world.

Cue Obama.

He has already unified this country through his intelligence, hope, stamina, compassion, and his willingness to speak the truth. By choosing a vice-president with the experience he lacks, Obama showed the country that he will surround himself with individuals who have everything America needs to get out from under the boot of George W. Bush.

Looking at the nation through a magnifying glass, equality is not revealed, especially since Bush has thrust us into debt and recession. There are great disparities in income and wealth among the classes; gaps within races, ethnicities, genders, and sexualities. Power remains in the hands of the few, not the majority. The time has come for change. It is time not not only for the candidate for change, but also for unification between political parties, skin color, and the sexes. Obama already has shown us that putting our differences aside is what we need for the betterment of the country as a whole.

While the fate of our economy is up in the air, January 20, 2009, instilled true hope for the near and distant future in the hearts of millions of Americans. After decades of electing a divisive president in some way, a large majority of us have chosen a man with the potential of being a great leader.

Yes we can? Oh no. Yes we did.

Alison J. Walkley is a reporter and freelance writer from Connecticut who has published in national magazines like Curve and The AFRican. After traveling to Malawi, Africa, with the Peace Corps upon graduation, she took a job writing for The Fairfield Citizen-News. Walkley is working on the publication of her first novel, Choice.

Godspeed, Mr. President

Hap Slattery

the Commander-in-Chief Ball: Reflections from a Combat Veteran.

Before beginning my story of how I had the opportunity to attend the Commander-in-Chief (CinC) Ball on Inaugural Day at the National Building Museum, I need to provide a concise history of how I came to be considered as an invitee. On September 11, 2001, I was a little over halfway into my four-year experience at West Point, and I would argue that no institution felt the ripple effect more from this event than West Point. Upon graduation in May of 2003, I accepted a commission in the U.S. Army as a Second Lieutenant, and I began my initial training as an infantry officer. While serving as a Vanguard in 1-18 Infantry, I spent the next four years abroad and deployed on two separate occasions to Iraq for a total of nearly two years. In May of 2008, I separated from the active-duty Army, moved back to New Jersey, joined a global consulting firm, and continued my service as a Captain in the New Jersey National Guard.

The week before Obama's inauguration was a typical work week. However, around noon on that Thursday, I received an email inviting me to attend the CinC Ball.

Initially, I thought it was "spam," but when I noticed that the email originated from the National Guard Bureau, I decided to respond. I got an immediate response confirming my attendance. On Friday, I made all of the pertinent arrangements for train tickets, a date, lodging and my uniform. On Saturday, FedEx delivered two tickets, and late Sunday evening, I boarded a train from Newark to Washington. Only 72 hours had passed since receiving that first email. On the way to DC, I was feeling apprehensive and unsure of exactly what drove me to follow through and make the trip. I had almost no clue what was to occur at this ball, but my gut instinct told me that I needed to be there.

Tuesday morning, I awoke in a DC suburb and watched President Obama take the oath on TV. I listened as he described our current economic and foreign diplomatic situation as a "raging storm." While the president and other dignitaries attended the swearing-in, the luncheon, and the parade, I headed to DC to reach my date's apartment. We arrived at the ball by 6:30 that night, and I began to gain a better understanding of the gravity of the CinC Ball. I first thought the ball was for Generals, Admirals, and the highest echelons of the military leadership; I saw quickly that the CinC Ball is actually a venue for "wounded warriors" and the family members of "fallen heroes."

The evening began around 7:30 with George Lopez as the Master of Ceremonies. By 8:00 pm, Vice President Biden stepped on to the stage and initiated a video teleconference with soldiers deployed to Tikrit, Iraq. The vice president went on to discuss some of his contributions to the Global War on Terror, and he ended his comments by saying that he was a proud father of a deployed service member and was looking forward to bringing some of the soldiers home.

After Vice President Biden made his graceful exit, Bon Jovi and Richie Sambora took the stage and played, "Who Says You Can't Go Home." Then President Obama took the main stage, began by acknowledging the 300 "Wounded Warriors" in attendance, and went on to initiate a second video teleconference with soldiers from the Illinois National Guard deployed to Afghanistan (most of whom were Cubs fans, much to the president's dismay). The president went on to extol those who have chosen to serve, and he outlined some of his responsibilities as Commander In Chief. President Obama and Michelle danced a bit, with two service members "cutting in," and they were on their way. Bon Jovi took over and played "Livin' on a Prayer" and closed with "Wanted Dead or Alive."

The crowd started to die down around 11 pm, but the "wounded warriors" were still enjoying the limelight. After all, it was their night. Admiral Mullen (Chairman of the Joint Chiefs of Staff), General Casey (Chief of Staff of the Army) and the senior non-commissioned officers of each of the services were entertaining questions and mingling with the crowd. Maybe it's difficult to imagine, but of the 300 wounded warriors, there were about 15 canes, 15 sets of crutches, 30 wheelchairs and only about 150 legs. Some had lost both, and others had lost portions of a limb or suffered burns that had caused a serious disfiguration. To me, that's what a hero looks like.

While I was walking through the crowd, I came across one wheelchair-bound "wounded warrior" that I will never forget. During my second tour, I was stationed in southern Baghdad. One night, after a memorial service for two soldiers that gave their last full measure, Lieutenant Colonel Gadson, a battalion commander for one of the field artillery battalions, was returning to Baghdad International Airport . His Up-Armored HMMW vehicle was struck by an Improvised Explosive Device causing the amputation of both of his legs from the knee down. I had never met him, but I was intimately familiar with the event. My unit had provided the assistance to allow LTC Gadson to be evacuated and helped to recover the hulk of the destroyed vehicle. Having the chance to see the president, vice president and all of the entertainers was of course an unforgettable experience, but the highlight of the evening was having the chance to introduce myself to LTC Gadson.

In the "blink of an eye," LTC Gadson was a double amputee, and in a similar fashion, President Obama became the President of the United States immediately following the swearing-in. Though our political situation and a personal situation can change dramatically, nothing in the military or society as a whole can change so rapidly. We can only hope that President Obama will follow through to achieve his vision of "Renewing America's Promise." Regardless of our politics, I think that we are all ready to assist and will support this endeavor to the best of our ability. Godspeed, Mr. President.

Hap Slattery is a former army officer and combat veteran who is currently working in management consulting in New York City.

Today

Daphne Uviller

i t's sometimes hard to separate my low expectations from the reality of Obama's superior qualifications. I wanted a president who can speak proper English, who doesn't act like a frat boy, who doesn't steal elections, who doesn't lie to get us into war, who doesn't blow a good economy (Clinton had us on track to be debt-free by the end of 2000–ha!), who isn't afraid to listen to people who don't agree with him. I could go on. The point is, Obama would be extraordinary, even if he followed a talented president. He is clear-eyed, honest (oh, please, I hope this is true), hardworking, ambitious on behalf of America, unafraid of the truth, ready for a challenge, erudite, thoughtful.

I am so excited for this day. I am elated that we have taken great strides in overcoming a shameful past. I am thrilled that I no longer have to pretend I am Canadian when I travel abroad.

Today, for the first time in eight dark years, I am proud to be an American.

Daphne Uviller is the author Super in the City, *a novel recently published by Bantam Dell. A former Books/Poetry editor at* Time Out New York, *her reviews, profiles, and articles have been published in* The Washington Post, The New York Times, Newsday, New York, *and* Self, *for which she used to write an ethics column. She is currently working on her next novel for Bantam.*

Dear Children and Grandchildren... I Remember

Jan Philpot

"I remember..." Those words have echoed through generation after generation of our family. For more than 200 years they have been recited by elders to descendants concerning affairs of this country. Most of the words have been lost in time, never written, never recorded. Some I know.

"I remember..." My great grandmother remembered a war-ravaged nation, brother spilling the blood of brother. She remembered the march of Union soldiers on her community, the battlefield strewn with torn bodies and the moans of those brothers and fathers, sons and neighbors. She remembered homes hastily converted into makeshift hospitals. I never heard her speak the words, but my grandfather told me of it.

"I remember..." My grandfather remembered the first airplane, automobile and telephone he ever witnessed. He remembered a first World War and the pain of losing a brother in it. He remembered the Depression and collective willing sacrifice. He remembered that Franklin Roosevelt did indeed begin "putting a chicken in every pot".

"I remember..." My mother remembered suffering on the homefront of World War II. She remembered harsh days of rationing coupled with willing sacrifice. She remembered the horror of film clips depicting a nightmarish Holocaust. She remembered traveling on a train north to south. At a certain point the conductor would announce loudly, "Mason-Dixon Line!" The "colored" would quietly rise and move to the back of the passenger car. She remembered "colored" and white restrooms and drinking fountains.

"I remember..." I too remember. I remember intense patriotism surrounding America's space program, John Glenn's first flight, the landing on the moon. I remember the icy fear of a Cold War and fallout shelter drills at school. I remember the assassinations of John F. Kennedy and Martin Luther King, and the confusion and stunned bewilderment in adults around me. I remember the anger surrounding Vietnam. I came of age during a time of upheaval and questioning, riots and protests. Our nation's leaders were viewed with distrust. Ideals upon which we were founded were mocked. Patriotism took a plunge from which it hasn't fully recovered.

I officially became a senior citizen in the same month of the same year that our first African-American president took office. I lived to see the hopeful ending of an old story of racial conflict. I see a nation marveling at how far we have traveled since the days my great grandmother looked upon a battlefield strewn with bleeding bodies. Our nation looks again with eyes of patriots at a leader stressing values of brotherhood and self-sacrifice. This confident man does not lie to us, but he agrees harder times are ahead. And I see in the shining tear-filled eyes of so many...hope.

Our first immigrant ancestor over 200 years ago also said "I remember..." and spoke of hope when his eyes lit on these shores.

I am your mother and your grandmother...and I remember.

Jan Philpot lives in Kentucky. She is a retired teacher and librarian, the mother of five and the grandmother of soon-to-be nine grandchildren. She does commissioned artwork, runs a campground for a living, and writes for fun.

Slainte, Mr. President.

James McShane

"What's on the TV?" Denny McGrath asks me. Lunch is over and the bar has gone quiet again. The smell of the chef's homemade leek and potato soup still lingers, though. Since the smoking ban came into force four years ago, a lot of smells are more noticeable now, including, unfortunately, Denny.

"Today's the big day," I say. "It's goodbye Bush, hello Obama." I switch over to Sky News and turn the sound up a notch. Billy over in the corner wakes up, the noise from the TV stirring him from his reverie. He blinks at the plasma screen, blinks again, then goes back to sleep, leaving his pint untouched.

"Oh, yes," Denny says with forced enthusiasm. "The invigoration is on now, isn't it?"

"Inauguration," I correct him, playfully. "The moment of change has arrived, or so they tell us.....change we can believe in. Great slogan, though."

"You forget something, James." Denny wraps his two hands around his Budweiser; the arthritis has become more pronounced as the weather gets colder.

"What's that?"

"This is Ireland. What business is it of ours what happens over in America? We're only a blot on the landscape compared to the United States. They don't care about us anymore. The days of JFK and Bill Clinton are all but gone."

I think about this for a minute; part of me agrees with what Denny is saying, but I have always had a fascination with the U.S. My family nearly moved to New Jersey in the late seventies, and I'll make my first trip to the states this summer. And no country—apart from, maybe, England does pageantry quite like America.

"Look at that, Denny," I say, gesturing to the TV. "See all those people in Washington? They are there to see one man. The last time we had anything like that over here was when the Pope visited. When was that?"

"I remember. It was 1979," Denny sighed. "I was in the Phoenix Park the day he said Mass."

"This is the same thing," I replied. "You can almost touch the hope these people feel. See all the colour, Denny? It's beautiful. There's a rumour going around that Obama might pay us a visit some time."

"He's supposed to have roots in County Offaly. I read that in one of the papers," Denny said. "It's a mighty spectacle all the same. You wouldn't see that happening for any of our leaders.... I'll have another pint when you're ready, James."

"Right you be, Denny." I fill up a fresh beer for him and pour a glass of Coke for myself.

The cheers erupt on the screen; Billy over in the corner stirs again, but doesn't open his eyes this time. Denny and I raise our glasses.

"Slainte, President Obama," I say. Good health.

"Go n'eirigh an bothar leat," replies Denny. May the road rise with you.

James McShane lives in Dublin, Ireland, and is studying journalism at the Dublin Business School. In his spare time, he bartends and toils on his first novel, The Dark Crusade of Robinson Stone.

Hussein

Brian Frederick

Hussein is the middle name of Barack Obama, the newest President of the United States of America. That just doesn't seem like that big of a deal to me. However, in the days leading up to the presidential election of 2008, it was that middle name in fact that so many people got hung up on. It seems that a rash group of people opposed to Barack Obama made his middle name a point of contention. Emails, flyers, and back-room whispers perpetrated rumors that Obama was not an American and was a radical Muslim, and many bought into it. No one believed this insipid idea more than my 70-year-old grandmother.

Hate is such a powerful and heartless beast. My grandmother could be considered old-fashioned and, to most people, deeply racist. She believed Obama had a "Muslim agenda," and she swore up and down that "they were taking over" and "we were without hope." Why were people so comfortable preaching this anger, this negligent hate-mongering? I have never been witness to such a fearful display of prejudice, and I pray I never will again. I was so afraid to say anything. I was paralyzed with fear when dealing with my grandmother, and others who felt the same way. Given our country's direction over the last few years, I found great joy in thinking that it all could be different. I bought into the idea of change. I didn't have it in my heart to not believe.

Hope swept over my world on November 4th, 2008, with the election of our new leader. After all of the drama, after all of the hatred, Barack Obama was elected president. People danced, tears fell, many an "AMEN" was shouted from main street windows. I was overwhelmed with optimism. All the bitter falsehoods were washed away by the power of the heart and mind.

Healing is what I was looking for in these days leading to January 20, 2009. I look at my grandmother—at other racists and pessimists—and want to erase their fears. Now that change, now that hope, now that Barrack Hussein Obama will be our president, I want the fearful to be strong. I want them to open their minds and listen. I want them to hear the truth like a calm, soothing medicine. We can do it! We CAN grow and prosper and remain the greatest country on Earth; not on a flimsy foundation of hate, but on a solid, sturdy foundation of hope and love.

Brian Frederick is a native Jersey boy who now resides in Tampa, Florida. He is an author, singer, and songwriter.

An Oath of Hope

Olajide A. Omojarabi

may 29, 1999, was a remarkable day in Nigeria when the first democratically elected president was sworn in. People, both young and old—in the middle of their grief of past military torture and unfavorable economic conditions—turned out in their numbers to see the outcome of their franchise for the first time. Although then, beyond my feeble comprehension, Nigerians couldn't stop being excited at finally being heard. Today, 10 years later, it's probably most gratifying to be among those nurturing Nigeria's nascent democracy. I have been very privileged to have America's democracy, in its autumn years, as my source of inspirations.

Jan 20 will of course unravel events that surpass a cogent inaugural speech and swearing-in ceremony. It is a reflective day set aside to honor the "great activists," those who fought for the emancipation of slaves and the liberation of the black race. It's a prospective day, believed by these brave men that America will once again be seen as the best last hope of earth. Here in Nigeria, the day should be set aside to commemorate the intense effort and deep sacrifice of those, who in the process of struggling for Nigeria's initiative and independence, lost their lives. For youths in Africa and beyond, the day will prove a promise kept and belief in a world where success is no longer attributed to the color of your skin or background but the content of your character. Jan 20, 2009, will remain one of America's most memorable days in history when Barack Obama will stand on Capitol's West and take the oath of office as the 44th President—and the first African-American to hold that post.

In recent months after Obama was announced president-elect, the Americans anticipated the day he would be swearing the oath of office, but obviously, they are not alone. From the deep corner of the developing world to exposed areas of advanced nations, the expectations are high. While the affluent minorities have the privilege of seeing the inauguration ceremony live, the underprivileged majority might not even have a TV set to watch this remarkable day in thatched-roof homes. These are the people whose inaugural preparation is based on wishes that their voices could be heard. They are parents who wish their children could be Ivy-league trained like Obama. They are bewildered children whose sunken eyes belie their starvation and plead for rescue. They're not far from us. In the streets, they are seen hawking, begging and crying of deprived joyful tendencies. In Africa, their empathy is no longer drawn from being poor but not being heard. They are the global citizens of the underprivileged world who wish and pray that the world they leave their children is better than the one they inhabit.

When the great activists of the world fought for freedom and equality, they did so with humility. Some fought religiously, others radically. In the end, they left behind imprinted confidence in their footsteps and sowed bravery in their hearts. However, these activists in their best interest saved these aspirations for better days, when the youths after them could take their inspiration further. Unfortunately, few leaders in the developing nations have been able to pass on these messages of hope. That is why youths in my country can't comprehend enough

the qualities of a man whose eloquence and charisma
won him a mantle of leadership to the White House.
Many inaugurations in Nigeria have occurred over the
years, and none has been persuasive enough to instill
confidence and nurture dreams for tomorrow's leaders.
Little wonder every college kid in Nigeria—from the
least educated to the highly learned—are now drawing
inspirations from Obama. While most youths in these part
of the world lack the benefits of leadership skills, their
counterparts in other developed countries are reaping
the dividends of focused leaders who swear an oath of
office not to get intoxicated by power but to serve as role
models in order to guarantee a fuller rewarding lives for
these youths—the leaders of tomorrow.

Across the globe, the inauguration of Obama as the 44th
American president reflects the course which the great
activists fought—for equal treatment and just laws. While
Reverend Martin Luther King, Jr., believed in a future
where there shall be one America, Abraham Lincoln's
dream was of a place and time when America will be
seen as the last best hope of Earth. Although, it was a
long-awaited dream, it has finally come true. Today, the
people of the world stand on their feet from Afghanistan to
Zimbabwe, in developed and developing world, to witness
the arrival of history in its making. That which will send
the true significance of inauguration to every home—from
blacks to whites, Latinos to Asians, poor to rich, and able
to disabled. An inauguration that will show that America's
greatness as reaffirmed by Obama is not based on the
height of its skyscrapers, or economic size, but summed
up in a declaration made over two hundred years ago.

While my aspirations for Nigeria are to work toward
achieving the dreams of its founding fathers, I hope to
share these dreams with fellow aspirants whose goal is
to reach a place and time when there shall be no more
leaders without vision and effort, without goals and

objectives. We seek leaders with hope and sacrifice.
Leaders who don't limit themselves to the views and
objectives of their past activists but also take the pains of
following the World as it lurches ahead.

82

*Olajide A. Omojarabi lives in Nigeria and loves reading
great short stories. His favorite authors are: Edgar Alan
Poe, Earnest Hemingway, Virginia Woolf, and Maya
Angelou. He is a student and currently at work on a
book project.*

Glass Half-Empty

William Tiernan

my dad's a "glass half-empty" kind of guy. Tell him you won a free vacation to Disney World and he'll remind you how long the line is for Space Mountain. He closely follows current events and politics with a Saint Bernard's scent for the scandalous; I swear he knew O.J. was going to jail before O.J. did, and I think he was in on the federal wiretapping of Rod Blagojevich. He votes Democratic, but only because the alternative is "worse." In the case of George W. Bush, "much, much worse."

But this election was different. My dad was pumped about Obama. He wore a red Obama trucker's hat and plastered his car with "Yes We Can" bumper stickers; daily he called me to make sure I was registered; he called friends he hadn't talked to in 10 years to remind them election day was November 4; and each political statement he made began with, "Not since Bobby Kennedy..."

He visited me and my wife on Halloween to take our 20-month old daughter trick or treating. The next day he collapsed from internal bleeding and had to be rushed to the hospital. The doctors—and about 12 blood infusions— saved him, but he was pissed.

"Dad, you're going to be fine," I said.

"No, I'm not," he said. "How am I going to vote from a

hospital bed?"

****

After Obama was elected my dad made sure his granddaughter knew the name of the president-elect. When he called, I handed the cell phone to Sophia, who gleefully stuck it to her ear.

"Who's going to be the next president?" I heard him ask.

"Say 'Obama' Sophia," I said. "Say, 'Obama'."

"Bamma!" she shouted. "Bamma!" She may have said "Mamma"—but my dad was satisfied.

He called again yesterday, immediately after Obama's inauguration speech. "Did she watch?"

Yes, she did. She sat in her highchair two feet from the television and watched the whole speech. When the crowd clapped, she clapped. When Obama made his final comment on protecting and delivering freedom to future generations, he received a standing ovation. Sophia stood in her chair, smiled, and smacked her hands together. "Yaaaaa! Yaaaaa!"

"Who is the president?" I asked.

"Bamma!"

She clapped again. It seems everyone had a reason to celebrate this day.

William Tiernan has two simple requests for President Obama: to make Sierra Mist Cranberry Splash the national drink, and to make all Fridays from now until the end of time national days of golf.

What Happened to My America?

Geri Spieler

my thoughts on the coming presidential inauguration take me back to the moment that I began to fear living in the United States.

In Philip Roth's novel, *The Plot Against America*, Charles Lindbergh beats out Franklin Roosevelt and is elected President of the United States in 1940. In the novel, Lindbergh negotiated a cordial accord with Adolf Hitler, accepting his conquest of Europe that created an atmosphere of anti-Semitism and bigotry. America became a nightmare for Jews, and the country became polarized politically as well as racially. Anyone found to be against the president was labeled instantly as a traitor.

How could this have happened? Why didn't someone do something?

I read that book in 2004. I had the uncomfortable feeling I was reading the history of the United States in 2005. Roth's book was supposed to be fiction, yet I shelved it under non-fiction.

The parallel to 2004 was uncomfortably close. We had a president who disregarded the laws of the land. He fostered divisions in the country and suppressed dissent of any kind. He allowed favoritism in his administration and permitted his military to make their own rules.

Why didn't someone do something? Why didn't I? And, more importantly, why didn't our Congress? Where were they? Why didn't they protect us from our version of Charles Lindbergh? Was there no one to speak for me?

Apparently not.

I am not yet hopeful. I'm looking for something I could not find for eight years: An opportunity to bring us back. I hope to move Roth's book to the fiction shelf.

Geri Spieler is the author of Taking Aim at the President, *the true story of Sara Jane Moore, the only woman to have attempted a U.S. Presidential assassination. Her new book, to be published by Macmillan, is hitting stores in early 2009. Spieler has written articles for the* Los Angeles Times, *was a featured correspondent for the* San Francisco Chronicle, *and was published in* Westways *magazine and* Forbes.

A Letter From Prison

Hope Henry

Who would have thought that on a bleak day in September a bunch of juvenile delinquents could be persuaded to work for a candidate running for president? As a teacher in a detention facility in southern Maryland, my students are a varied patchwork of felons. Somewhere along the line each of these young men, mostly black, managed to slip through the No Child Left Behind promises of George Bush and his cronies.

Anger and resentment greet me each morning as I welcome the young men back to class. We greet one another and then begin a range of discussions on what each of us can do with our critical thinking skills to improve our lives and further our careers. On that particular drab day in September, the students entered class with vacant stares, intermittent jabbering and a sense of nonchalance. None of this bothered me as I stood up from behind my desk and greeted each newcomer to the unlit room. "Today we are going to write a letter to someone", I said, introducing the lesson to the hardened stares of students, most of whom have been educated on the streets and have minimal interest in learning.

"You have five minutes to write to Mr. Obama about your dreams for your life and your request for what you would like to get out of your life." The students groaned but I knew that they believed I would mail their letters and that perhaps they would be answered. I know also that their lives of poverty have left them with little hope, low self esteem, and a disbelief in the words, "Yes, we can." Nonetheless, the students pushed ahead with their letters in order to complete the task and possibly to say something of importance.

At the end of class Daquan, a 15-year-old African-American walked up to my desk with a scrawled note and told me that I could send this letter to Mr. Obama and maybe he would read it to his daughters. Here is what he wrote:

Obama,

We are the forgotten. My mother told me that when I grow up I can be something big. But when I walk out of my house I see only drug pushers and gangsters. We live behind the White House. Nobody like you comes to see how we live. I go to school and the same teacher is not in my class. The students, we are poor. We have nothing. The streets are our life. How can you fix this Obama? I want to go to school. I want to be something when I grow up. I am not a lottery ticket. I am a boy with hopes and dreams. Please help us Mr. Obama. I know that my teacher here tells me you will read my letter. Maybe you visit here. Please don't leave us behind when you make this change and get this hope.

Daquan.

Inauguration Day 2009: A Conversation with My Kids

Rebecca Wilson-Shore

On Tuesday, January 20th, I drove my three children (my 7-year-old daughter and 5-year-old twin sons) to elementary school having the following conversation:

Me: "Hey guys; ya know what is special about today? We are getting a new president."

Twin 1: "Is it Barack Obama?'

Me: (Smiling now) "Yes, it is."

Twin 2: (Looking at Twin 1 with big eyes) "Ooooh. It is Barack Obama."

Daughter: "I already knew that."

Nonchalance. It humored me that the significance of this day was lost on her. She lives with no idea how many broken backs have borne the weight of oppression, yet still raised themselves up to amble forward—bent and bleeding—in the struggle for this day to become a reality. A day when a man of color can sit in the highest seat in this great country.

For my 7-year-old, it was no more notable that this year's presidential race was a battle including an African-American man and a middle-aged woman than it would have been if two paunchy, middle-aged white men were running... as usual. She sits in school amidst as many African-American and Mexican-American children as white boys and girls. And, when helping me put names to faces in the effervescent second-grade world of "who's who," she usually describes her friends to me as, "the one with the yellow hair, or the one with the brown or black hair, the one with lots of freckles, and the one more tan than me or the one with darker skin." Just as often, she'll say, "you know, the one who always wears purple, or the one with the green striped skirt sitting with me in car-line today." She gives as much descriptive credit to skin color as to what color sneakers a kid has or what is written on his or her jacket.

She hasn't been poisoned with the negative terminology that too often becomes the dirty filter through which many adults would see and subsequently name her little school friends. At this point in her young life, they are one thing to her: her friends.

After school, I picked them up and asked if they saw the inauguration at school. "YES" they all belted out together. Their voices overlapped in their excitement. "In the lunchroom." "We saw it on TV." "We all clapped when the people on TV clapped." "Do we have a new president now?"

Me: (Smiling again) "Yes, we do."

Twin 1: "I'm gonna be president when I grow up."

Me: (Grinning now) "And why not?!"

Anything is possible. Anything at all.

Rebecca Wilson-Shore is a mother of three from Florida. She originally emigrated to the U.S. from Leeds, England at the age of eight. She has been writing since she was 10 years old.

For Me, It All Started in New Orleans

Tim Danos

"he's going to help us," she said. So said my brother-in-law's mother on July 21, 2006, when Barack Obama came to visit New Orleans.

In the aftermath of Hurricane Katrina, New Orleans, the place of my birth, was devastated; the infrastructure was in shambles, people fled their homes, the economy was in peril, and there was a general desperation for signs of hope and progress.

During a summer vacation, I traveled from Washington to New Orleans to visit my family and volunteer for Habitat for Humanity to rebuild homes in the Ninth Ward. For several weeks, I helped build homes in an area of the Ninth Ward called Musician's Village, a housing community for low-income musicians.

Every Friday afternoon, the homeowners performed music for the volunteers, who had come from all walks of life; every age, race, religion, sexual orientation, and socioeconomic status. On this particular Friday, Sen. Barack Obama, a rising star in the U.S. Senate, came to visit our work site as he toured around the Gulf Coast. Sen. Obama sat on the front bench of an in-progress house, smiling and stomping his right foot to the music, and all of us enjoyed it as well. This was a glimpse of an America that I hoped to see in my lifetime—a sense of unity in a time of great divisiveness.

Following the performance, I approached Sen. Obama to thank him for his work. I asked him if he would record my outgoing voice mail message on my cell phone. He agreed to do it, and for the longest time, until I switched carriers, my voice mail played, "Hi, this is Tim's phone. He's not here right now, so leave him a message and he'll be sure to get back in touch with you. Bye Bye." I called everyone I knew and told them about it, with most of them having no idea who Barack Obama was.

And so, almost two and a half years later, Barack Obama is the President of the United States of America. He faces the same difficulties as presented in New Orleans: an infrastructure in need of correct and long-term repair, rising home foreclosures, an economy in a period of recession, and a citizenry desperate for signs of hope and progress.

The journey that started in New Orleans continues today. I believe he's going to help us, and that's good. That's really good.

Tim Danos, 21, lives in Chevy Chase, Maryland, and is a student at Washington College in Chestertown, MD.

The Peaceful Transfer of Power

Cassandra Nye

Like so many others I was moved by this election from the early stages. Moved by how my generation discarded complacency and joined together to fight for change, moved by the passion stirred up by a Senator from Illinois and his vision for America, and moved by the history that was being made as we voted the nation's first African-American president into office.

Yet, standing on the Mall on January 20, 2009, I was not prepared for how moved I would be by the phrase that describes inauguration day in its most simple form, which is "the peaceful transfer of power."

Here we are in a time when partisan politics run rampant; at a time of war that–at its core–is a struggle for power, a time when our powerful economy seems less-so, and some have even gone so far as to question our position as a world "superpower." I was overwhelmed by how incredibly proud I felt to I live in a country where the least popular outgoing president in recent history was able to shake hands and peacefully transfer "power" to the much-more-popular president-elect. No struggle, no battle, just a celebration of where we can go as a nation–indicating a love of country that is perhaps greater than a love of power. I know it's not as simple as that, but for a moment it seemed so.

And in the moments after power was transitioned and so much of what has moved me over the past year came to fruition, I felt truly honored to be among the two million or so people who showed up just to celebrate the inauguration. Whatever my fellow attendees' reasons for spending the money it took to get there, taking the time to make the trek, braving the cold, and dealing with the crowds (and all the while keeping a smile on their faces), I was glad to share in it. I have rarely felt such a unity between people from all walks of life, and my hope is that a bit of that shared experience will stay with us as we go back to the day-to-day and work to fix the many problems knocking on our respective—and collective—doors. It was moving, exciting, and it felt right to be hopeful.

Cassandra Nye lives in New York City and works in public relations. Her spare time is spent with her urban family and usually involves consuming some sort of wine and a variety of cheese-like substances.

Distant, Present

Matthew Frederick Griffin

i was time zones away from the U.S. when the November election results were declared, up all night refreshing news websites at dial-up speeds. When I returned to New York City later that month, I was determined to celebrate with friends at the "answering" moment, when the transition became official and binding.

I called D.C. friends to secure a patch of floor and a volunteer slot to put me in the thick of things. But it wasn't to be. I greeted the top of the year by collapsing under eight days of the worst flu I have ever suffered. I called my host in DC and croaked, "I'm sick, I'm so wiped. Help."

"Don't worry," she chirped. "You've been upgraded to the sofa!" Rumors circulated of individuals renting studio apartments for tens of thousands of dollars, and my friend had for me an entire sofa? "But," I said, "my ride canceled on me." Silence. "And I have the flu." Silence.

"Matt," she asked. "Do you need to cancel?" Silence from my side of the line.

I called New York friends, throat and head fuzzy and imprecise, and sought alternative plans. Friends were non-committal, or else so carefully pre-ticketed that I had no hope to join them. So I went up to Columbia University to join the thousands of undergrads, grads, professors, alumni, and staff gathered sheepishly on the damp stone and brick of the courtyard in front of the Lowe Library to cheer at an outdoor screen and sound system.

On the screen as I arrived: a procession of vehicles, crowds cheering, arriving dignitaries announced. Me: I surveyed the crowd searching for familiar faces and finding only strangers.

C-SPAN's awkward, amateur live-switching and close-caption gaffes helped boost morale as the New York audience struggled to figure out how we were meant to engage this distant screaming crowd on the video system. We could chuckle together, and that helped us get a sense of one another. But were we participants or observers? Did our remote location allow us to respond with more candor than courtesy suggested to the specific people selected by the cameras, or was more sobriety demanded of us? When members of the Bush family and core administration appeared on screen, there was a dampening of all voices in the crowd, followed by uneasy laughter.

And as the official ceremony began—I found my friends—all questions of our behavior vanished as the crowd collectively entered into the screen, transported into a one-to-one relationship with that distant place. Our crowd after all was simply a patch of that crowd—our voices a slice of that chorus.

"I'm terrified," I told a friend, "But thankfully this is really happening."

"It is happening," my friend said. "I can't feel my toes, but I feel different already than I did five minutes ago. Keep this going, keep this all happening."

Matthew Griffin is a writer, producer, and film editor living in New York City. He will complete his MFA in Writing (Fiction) from Columbia University in May 2009. At present, he is working to complete his first novel and a collection of stories.

A Few Words From a Southern Gentlemen

Melanie Rae Bertenshaw

i am conveying a few words from my friend Curtis Brown:

Curtis is a true southern gentleman. A 50-year-old man of color who never thought he would see the day of an African-American president. He jotted down a few thoughts as he watched Obama take the oath of office…

"I will do all things through Christ who strengthens me. I am a man of color whose daughter-in-law just gave birth to my first grandson. This is a great time for me! A new president who looks like me! A new grandson! As I watch the prayer service at the inauguration, I am in tears. There is nothing wrong with a man shedding a few tears. I feel like a man today. A man with hope. A man of color. A man who isn't afraid to cry."

Melanie Rae Bertenshaw, 44, grew up In Lincoln, Rhode Island, and has been living in Virginia for the past eight years. She came to writing late, but is now a stay-at-home writer who sells vintage clothing on Ebay.

I Witnessed History and My Dogs Didn't Care

Kevin Cline

i sat on the worn couch in my living room, one dog on my lap, the other on the floor beside me. When Barack Hussein Obama raised his hand to take the oath, I tried to impress on them the gravity of the moment, but they slept on, unimpressed. Honestly, they could not care less about such things. I talked to them anyway, "Don't you guys realize what this means? This is huge! My God, look at all those people. I don't ever remember anything like this. This is so unreal."

The dog draped across my lap opened one eye and looked at me. "Don't you want to watch?" I asked her. The eye closed and she sighed, annoyed that I had the nerve to disturb whatever dream she was having.

My attention went back to the TV. When the oath, a constitutional verse, was messed up, I smiled. When the faintest smile touched the corners of the president's mouth, I laughed. Suddenly, this historical moment became so much more: The unreal has become real.

The man taking this office, the highest office in America,

became one of us. This wasn't a man who would hide behind his desk and his people. He would do everything in his power to not lie to us; to not treat us as though we were his subjects, only existing to do his bidding while he made his deals and rewarded his friends. He would try not to get young people killed unnecessarily or to settle old grudges. He would neither bow to religious extremists, nor fight to make people different than him a lower class of citizen. He would embrace diversity and use it to make the country stronger.

He at once became the most powerful, and most common, man in America. In that tiny smile, he got the joke. He discovered the absurdity of the moment buried in all the pomp of circumstance.

I, along with untold numbers of people, burst into applause after "So help me God." For the first time, both dogs jumped to their feet staring at the TV, their ears raised, their heads cocked to the side, trying to figure out what this tremendous noise was. Soon, they realized they just didn't care. One went back to sleep and the other wandered off to get a drink of water.

Me? I was finally ready to believe in a president, THIS president; this man. Unlike the dogs, I stared rapt and fully awake, waiting for what he would say when he stepped up to the podium and into the sunlight.

Kevin Cline lives in North Ridgeville, Ohio, with his partner, Dan. They have two dogs (Sadie and Doogan), two cats (Mac and Ripley), a sugar glider (Satine), a parakeet (Juan), and a bunch of turtles.

Etched in Snow

Katie Krum

the day before the inauguration, I stomped down the stairs of my apartment building, bundled and braced for the cold. Snow had fallen the night before, padding the city and muting the regular hustle and bustle that scurried past. The air was crisp and quiet. I cut through the scene like a scissor, interrupting the vertical pattern of the cars and pedestrians in the middle of my block. As I crossed, I noticed the word "CHANGE" etched in snow across the side windows of a Civic parked on the far side of the street.

I smiled.

Perhaps it was someone tumbling out of the bar the night before, or maybe a high-school student on his way to school, maybe it was even someone who works at the FOX News building across the street from my apartment. Okay, maybe not, but it is possible, and that is what's so amazing.

Collective history is often marked by war and conflict. For some reason the positive parts of our timeline (beyond winning a war or ending a conflict) are lost in our recounting. Perhaps "collectively" the positive points in time are harder to agree on.

Not today. Anyone...anyone could have etched the word CHANGE. More importantly, we collectively created and witnessed the beginning of new possibilities. We etch "JANUARY 20, 2009," as an amazing, hopeful day in our collective history.

Katie Krum lives in New York City in a 300-square foot apartment. Originally from Bethlehem, Pennsylvania, she is used to corn fields and steel mills, but she has become quite fond of public transportation and $1.50 hotdog stands. Katie enjoys outdoor dining, fountain soda, and traveling to see friends.

You Have the Floor, Mister President.

P. S. Wigeland

On the night of November 4, 2008, I did not stay up late and watch the returns. I did not speculate on what would happen if by chance the "other guy" won. I didn't do any of those things because I knew Barack Obama would win as surely as I knew the sun would rise the next morning.

The people of Chicago and Illinois knew Barack Obama long before the nation got an up-close-and-personal look at him. He was our Senator. He cut his teeth on the Chicago politics that put him in the Senate. He came across, even then, as a quiet man with a thoughtful expression that led you to believe his mind never stopped working.

When he began his pursuit of the White House, I think even then I knew it was a foregone conclusion that only needed the rubber stamp of the American people at election time. Barack Obama exhibited all the elements of great presidents.

I have my personal list of great presidents from

this century: Franklin Roosevelt, John Kennedy, and William Clinton. I have seen presidents lost to history and remembered when it happened: John Kennedy's assassination, Richard Nixon's impeachment, George W. Bush's legacy. I knew the morning of November 5, 2008, when the election results were posted and pictures of the new president-elect hit the newsstands that it would be a noted milestone in history.

Americans are hard on their presidents. We expect perfection and forget they are only human. We want miracles and complain when events do not support our own interest. We age our Presidents with our demands, and we never apologize.

I look at the face of a young Barack Obama and wonder how the accelerated aging process will treat him. I wonder if he fully understands how the hope of millions rest on his shoulders, and if he does, how that will affect him. I wonder if the millions hoping for super-human solutions fully understand that this is a man leading us, and if they do, will they be supportive and patient?

The world has changed since I was a child. The greatest worry we had at the time was Communism and Russia. If only that were our greatest worry now.

The world is changing, and only history will tell whether it is for the better. But, the key words here are "the world" is changing, and America needs a leader that will change with the world.

America elects its greatest leaders when needed.

You have the floor, Mister President. We are listening.

P. S. Wigeland lives inthe Chicago area works for a construction company.

Amid My Children

John DeStefano

Amid the diapers and the toys,
the peanut butter sandwiches,
the pre-school chatter and the singing,

the guttural grunts and groans
Above it all; above those tiny voices,
Voices
many and from everywhere
yet all for one

One who introduced and corralled them all,
ranted, exasperated, and swore in all dialects,
One who sang with the gift of grace
a song of beauty that lacked a single voice,
One for whom all voices sang,
who spoke for us all in lieu of himself,
One who painted a watercolor diorama
with crayons and a pencil,
One who drew those colors into the faces of many

And all of it a dream--
of a dream and a dream come true--

And then: back to those tiny voices,
a stark re-entry into reality
    almost the same as before
    yet with something different:
    with a smile, and with hope
        in a dream

*John S. DeStefano Jr. is an engineer in the physics
department at Brookhaven National Laboratory, where he
writes technical information and works with web-based
technology. He lives in New York with his wife, Jody, and
their four children: Benjamin, Zachary, Sophia, and Jacob.*

Loving Today

Shannon O Neil

"Why?" He asks. I pause for a moment trying to dumb down the enormity of today into one powerful, meaningful sentence that might get my four-year-old excited to put four layers of clothes on and walk for miles and miles.

"Well," I start. "Even though it is a little cold and there will be a lot of people down there." (I purposefully leave out the part about the possibility of crazy people trying to do terrible things to people they have never seen). I remind him how I wished I had taken him to the inaugural concert on Sunday; how he would have loved the music and the way people of all ages and races and sizes were like one.

"Do they have toys there?"

"Um, where? You mean at the inauguration? I don't know honey, but we have to go. We just have to."

"I don't really want to go."

"Ok, give me three good reasons why you do not want to go, and we will go from there."

"Well, one it's cold. Two, there are going to be SO many people there and, and, and, and…three there are no toys there."

I mean, I practically spoon-fed him those first two excuses. I scramble and try a different approach.

"Ok so here is the thing, do you know what is happening today?"

"I know, I know. Barack Obama is going to be President."

"Right. What do you know about him?"

"Well, he has dark skin like me. And his friend Joe...he has light skin like you."

"Right and let me just explain this to you. See, for a long, long time, people never thought that someone with dark skin could ever be President. But they were wrong, very wrong. So, today we are celebrating the fact that anyone can be whatever they want to be. Today is like proof."

"Ok. Let's go." Just like that, he changed his mind and hopped up to get ready.

We layered up and headed out. My son, the perennial dawdler, walked idly to the metro, cheeks rosy from the chill. I had no idea what to expect–how he would handle the crowds, the excitement.

We spend hours in DC. We walk, we laugh, and we clap. We listen to the entire speech in silence. We have a great time. There is no whining, no crying, an occasional piggy-back ride, but otherwise the type of day that makes you feel like mother of the year. "Look at my son," I want to shout. He is really listening to this speech, he really gets it. I am daydreaming, seeing his face where Barack now stands. I am silently gloating. He'll thank me for this one day, he'll remember we came, he'll feel what this means. This is good.

We had a few casualties today...the favorite winter hat with the glow-in-the-dark skulls, the dropped pretzel, and of course the white Obama flag that made it until the split second before we stepped onto the Metro. Still, we are unfazed by the losses because we are on a complete high. I am still amazed at the way Trey hung in there today.

On the Capital Crescent Trail walking home, I thank him. Positive reinforcement from a first-time "super mom."

"That was a great day," I say. "I had such a great time with you, and I am so glad we went."

"Yes." He replies. "And it is such an important day."

"It is. I knew you would understand that more when we got down there." I am so happy I could turn around right there and take him out for a "backwards dinner" (ice cream sundae first then something healthy if he has room).

"Yeah, it taught everyone we can be whatever we want to be."

"Right, it's pretty cool to know that, huh?"

"Yeah. So I want to be Batman but I want to be able to use my Ben 10 watch to switch to different guys like whenever I want. So I want to be Batman and then I will switch to be Spiderman when I want to be him. Then..."

Shannon O'Neil works at an interactive patient care company in the Washington D.C. metro area. She hopes that when her son grows up, he'll wonder what all the fuss about race was about when his mom was a kid.

The Last Time...

Sarah Garcia

i rolled over and sighed, burying my face in the pillow. I could hear my sister talking—much too cheerfully for this early in the morning—to my mom as she flitted around the house trying to get ready for work. My dad had already told me to wake up, but I was taking my time. I inwardly groaned at the thought of leaving my sanctuary of warm pillows and blankets, but rolled out of bed anyway. I made my way to the next best place.

My dad was standing next to his large bed watching the small TV he had installed there only a few weeks ago. My sister sat on the edge of the bed halfway watching our mom run in and out of the room, halfway paying attention to the television.

"Whaa's goin' on?" I murmur as I fall onto the soft bed and curl up, nodding to the TV.

"Inauguration." My sister answers promptly.

"Oh," I rub my eyes, not completely awake, "Right."

We are silent for a few minutes as we watch the event taking place miles away. Even my mom stops her hectic morning ritual to sit on the bed and watch.

"The last time we were all sitting around the TV like this," my dad breaks the silence, "this early in the morning, was the Twin Towers..."

"Mm hmm," my mom agrees softly.

"Yeah," I sigh as I close my eyes, attempting to immortalize this moment in my memory.

"History in the making," was my sister's input.

Sarah Garcia, 15, lives in California and is into reading, writing, dancing, and playing the piano (though she hates reading the music).

The Poll Troll

John Meils

i t got worse as the election neared. I spent hours every day going from website to website, watching for the slightest changes in the polls. Each fluctuation, no matter how small, sent me into a minor panic or a small fit of joy. At first, I watched Ohio and Florida compulsively. Each had recently delivered a Presidency and I was sure it'd be the same this time. But there were others—Virginia, Pennsylvania, Colorado, Missouri, Nevada, New Mexico—and they were all in play. The combinations were crucial, pieces of an ever-changing puzzle I re-assembled daily.

The number "270," the electoral total needed for victory, became mythic. If Obama won the same states as Kerry did in 2004, plus Colorado, Nevada and New Mexico, he was good to go. He didn't need Florida or Ohio, though either could instantly put him over the top. But the polls—Gallup, Real Clear Politics, Rasmussen, Quinnipiac, take your pick—they all said something different and they were all in and out of the margin of error depending on the day of the week. Nothing was definitive, no lead was safe, no deficit insurmountable. Somehow Obama locked up Iowa early and that was good, but it only had seven electoral votes, the same as Connecticut. Michigan (17 electoral votes) would help, but couldn't seal the deal on its own.

North Carolina (15 electoral votes) would be a sweet prize, but the state hadn't gone for a Democrat in a national election since 1964.

I kept a calculator by my desk and furiously punched out scenarios a few times a day. I wasted countless hours, my freelance stock-in-trade, to insure that this election wouldn't be subject to the chicanery of the prior two. I discovered the electoral map on Politico.com, a beautiful tapestry of blue and red, red and blue, that encouraged constant recalculation. There were others like me, polls trolls, hundreds of thousands of us. We became the subject of news stories. Doctors were consulted about the relative health of our sudden obsessions.

I stumbled onto www.fivethirtyeight.com, the crack to my newly formed addiction. The site tracked all the polls and seemed to mix them magically together in combinations that both dazzled and perplexed. The homepage read like code in The Matrix; once you learned to "see" it, the picture became clear. Obama was going to win. The numbers didn't lie. Still, I pored over them daily as November arrived. All of us did, the poll trolls, the unofficial army of election observers.

On November 4th, it happened swiftly and early in the evening. The polls hadn't lied like they did in the past. Obama won handily, and there was much rejoicing. The next morning, I got up and cycled through the news sites and sports blogs I had read before the election. I didn't consult a single poll, and I experienced zero withdrawal from my addiction. I had been cured. We all had. It happened the moment Obama walked on stage in Chicago the night before.

OBAMA - A Canadian Perspective

Jim Swettenham

t ears of joy and excitement flowed as I attempted to swallow the lump that formed in my throat when I watched Inauguration Day ceremonies unfold for the 44th President of the United States of America—Barack Hussein Obama.

My six-year-old grandson joined me as we assembled a die-cast metal model car that I had given him for Christmas. I told him that we would assemble it on a very special day, not realizing that that special day would also be a historic one—not only for the American people—but for all the people of the world.

An astute young Christian, my grandson was impressed with the opening prayer offered by Pastor Rick Warren, as we watched CNN's Inauguration Day coverage from the comfort of my Winnipeg, Manitoba, living room. I attempted to explain to him the historic significance of the day as he tried to grasp the progress that had been made in overcoming racial differences in the world. He was puzzled when I pointed out Senator Edward Kennedy and told him about the assassinations of members of the Kennedy clan and Rev. Martin Luther King, Jr.

My ongoing concerns and prayers for President Obama have been that people will be patient with him, that they will realize that he is not the Messiah and that he does not walk on water. I was grateful that his humanity showed when he stumbled slightly during the taking of his oath of office.

President Obama has been stressing the fact that the changes that he had campaigned on and the changes that will be realized will not happen within the first 100 days of his administration. They will likely not be achieved within the first year or two, possibly not even within his first term, but he was confident enough to state that the goals would be met.

There has been some concern about the possibility of the Obama administration going into a protective mode and turning its back on its neighbors, but during his inaugural speech the president reiterated that "America is a friend of all nations" and in that moment fears of protectionism were, in my mind, dispelled.

Can the United States of America live through the days of change? Yes it can, especially under the watch of President Obama, who will receive guidance from God in whom he trusts.

God Bless President Obama and God Bless the United States of America. God can also bless Canada while He is at it.

Jim Swettenham is a semi-retired former journalist, firefighter, and rodeo broadcaster who currently resides in Winnipeg, Canada.

Letter to My Sons

Betsy Reymond

d ear Boys,

An amazing and wonderful thing happened last week. Our country elected a mixed-race man to be our president. I want to take a minute to tell you how I feel about it and to give you some historical perspective from our family's experience.

I'm beside myself with pride for the citizens of this country. I honestly didn't think that we had come this far. I expected a great concession speech from Mr. Obama and whatever would come after. I have never been so happy to be proven wrong! The positive consequences of this event will be impossible to quantify. All people benefit when any one of us reaches the goal of becoming the best he or she can be. When that goal is to be of service to his fellow man, the benefit is multiplied exponentially.

My hope for you is that you take Mr. Obama as a role model.

He exemplifies qualities that I want to see growing in each of you. I admire and value his even-handed

emotional expression, his generous nature that leads
him to serve, his humble self-assuredness, his devotion
to family, his respect for the opinion of others (even
when it differs from his own), his ability to really listen
to dissenting opinion and to make adjustments when
he recognizes a wrong turn, and last but not least his
dedication to treat his opponents with respect. These
aren't just admirable qualities, they are smart. We can
achieve our goal by living in a way that allows us to look
in the mirror every morning and feel pride. That is my
definition of real success.

On the subject of family history, here is a story to help
you gain some perspective:

I remember my Mother—your Grandmother, who was
born in 1923—telling me that when her Grandmother was
born (my guess would have been in about 1875), she was
given a slave as a gift. A little girl who was to serve her in
any way she wished. I believe that they lived in Tennessee
at the time. Those are all the details that she gave. That
was just 133 years ago and only four generations. Last
week, Ben and I and 52% of our citizens voted for a black
man who won the presidency of the United States. If that
doesn't define phenomenal, I don't know what does.

While I am clearly thrilled by this historic moment,
I'm also realistic. Our country has so many problems
to deal with. We will experience a lot of challenges and
difficulties in the next several years. However, I am so
glad that you are coming of age when we have so much
to be grateful for, we have so much to be proud of, and
we have so much to aspire to. You are fortunate to be
able to see history being made, and I charge you with
the responsibility to respond to the needs of your fellow
man and find ways, large and small, to be of service. That
is part of your heritage as well. Your Grandmother Mary

Helen would want you to know that to be of service is the pinnacle of human existence and experience.

Enjoy this moment.

Life is good.

I love you.

Mom

Betsy Reymond is from Texas and took her three sons Ben, 20, David, 17, and Mark, 14, to the inauguration and had a wonderful time.

Race to the White House

Matthew David Stevens

If you think racism is gone in this country, you're wrong. It's sad to say that, but it's true. I'm a 27-year-old white male, and I was extremely happy on Election Day. I remember the day very clearly. I was on break at work, sitting in the cafeteria watching Obama's election speech. In my opinion, it was very uplifting and inspirational. I know that actions speak louder than words (my co-workers were happy to point that out), but I felt ready for the change he was speaking of. I think we all are.

It was ten minutes before I had to go back to work and I decided to go take care of my nasty habit of smoking. I was standing outside listening to my fellow smokers' conversations, just taking it all in. What I heard made me angry. I know most of them were just blowing smoke (no pun intended), but the things they were saying were hurtful to a country that needs to change. How can we change this country, if we can't change ourselves?

Some of the jokes and comments went as follows:

"Pretty soon the whites are going to be the minority." (Maybe true, but does it matter? Maybe we already are. This has nothing to do with Obama.)

"He's going to be assassinated!" (Also could be true. There are a lot of angry racists that only see color or care about their own bank accounts instead of helping others.)

"He's a terrorist and is going to take us down from the inside." (This is just funny and it shows the ignorance of some people in this country.)

"He only cares about the black community. That's why he wants to help the poor." (This comment has to be the most racist one out of them all. I wonder if the person who said that even knew how racist it was. Not all blacks are poor. There are just as many white people living off of welfare and food stamps. Besides, do they forget he had a white mother?)

There were plenty of other comments like this, but no reason to go on. It just amazes me that people can be so hypocritical. We all want change and whoever helps us get there (no matter the color of their skin) is fine with me, because on the inside we are all just humans, trying to survive.

Matthew David Stevens is happily married and has two handsome sons. He typically likes to write fiction and also music.

The People's Inauguration

Josh Boxerman

Listening to President Barack Obama (even the sound of that name gives me chills) deliver his Inaugural Address, I marveled at his eloquence. As the Daily Show's Aasif Mandvi said the night before the Inauguration, his speech made "sweet love to the English language." Or, as my dad rather less eloquently put it, "Guy can really put words together."

This collection of words will not be nearly as eloquent as the one delivered on the steps of the Capitol on that historic day. But I would like to try to convey some of the emotion I felt, and that the people around me felt.

It really is impossible to describe the feeling in the air. There was so much love and energy and good feeling that no train delays or waiting in line or 20-degree temperatures could tamp it down. Everyone was upbeat, cracking jokes, and generally marveling that, yes, this is really happening and that, yes, we really are here to be a part of it.

Let me put it this way: It took something really special to get this many people, that happy, that early in the day, at that temperature.

Or as the president (oh man!) would put it: Hope was in the air. In the air, on the horizon, on the Mall and most importantly--on the steps of the Capitol. Anywhere it could find a spot to nestle and work its magic. You could see it in the faces of the people around you. Their eyes had a sparkle; there was a spring in their step that maybe wasn't there before.

There was also the sense that, because of this—because of the extraordinary political season that we had just lived through, because of the millions of disenfranchised brought into the political process—that this wasn't just the inauguration of a man to the highest office of a country. It was more than that. This inauguration was as much about the People of the United States of America as it was the new President of the United States of America. As he said on election night, "This is your victory." And it was our Inauguration.

When Barack Hussein Obama stood before us to take that sacred oath, I took a look around. All eyes were on the man, rapt. There were many expressions—most, of elation. Many, of disbelief. Some were just overcome by it all. An African-American couple to my right embraced and held up sheets of laminated paper—family trees, tracing their history right back to Africa. Just like their new president. Our new president.

Then, like thunder rolling from the hilltops, came the chant.

O-BA-MA! O-BA-MA! O-BA-MA! O-BA-MA! O-BA-MA!

And it would have continued. We would have gone on for hours had the occasion presented itself. But our new president held up his hand.

I have never heard two million people get so quiet.

"It's been a long, long time coming/But I know a change gonna come, oh yes it will." -- Sam Cooke.

Josh Boxerman, 15, hails from Maryland and is a sophomore in high school. He is the co-captain of the debate team, the assistant news editor of his school newspaper, and a huge fan of the Chicago Cubs and the Washington Nationals.

A Great Day

Mary Earhart

my son and his wife have a sick baby in the hospital, which translates into my babysitting their other two children. The boys are four and two. Edan loves to play video games and can beat me anytime. Taran is just learning to use the potty. I'm a pretty happy Grandma, ready to help out, but this is January 20th, 2009! Nearly a decade of bad decisions is behind the U.S.A. and I, for one, will no longer be embarrassed when foreign dignitaries visit Washington.

No, you can't watch cartoons. No, honey, I'm sorry but Grandma really wants to watch this man speak. After that I'll do anything you want to do, even play your Spiderman game.

And then Obama was at the podium. He was beginning to speak of what we as a nation have accomplished and what we can and must achieve by working together.

Edan wanted to tell me something. Taran was clearly interjecting "Poo-poo! Poo-poo!"

"Sshhh!" I said. "Just a minute!"

And I got a miracle (as any parent knows). They were quiet while Barack Obama shared his words...I didn't miss it. The cable didn't go out, my arms and legs didn't fly off, my head didn't explode. I heard it. I was moved to tears.

"What's the matter, Grandma?" Edan asked.

"Nothing's the matter, dear, I'm just very proud of our country today."

Taran again chimed in, "Poo-poo!"

Mary Earhart is a retired midwife who does most of her writing at a beach house in Costa Rica. She and her husband spend lots of time visiting their seven children and nine grandchildren in California.

Lincoln Penny Heads Up

Jaye Maynard

his morning I left my apartment in Hell's Kitchen, NYC, en route to the bus (which I take about once or twice a week). There it was at my feet, heads up. I might have passed it by, but it seemed to be smiling up at me on this day of all days when a self-proclaimed Abraham Lincoln mentee was to be sworn into office.

I wish I had been able to attend the inauguration on some level, to be one of the minions on the Mall, or a lucky buyer of a scalped $250 ticket, or an attendee of a ball, but that was not to be. I am a self-employed, uninsured, single, hard-working creative New Yorker, and I needed to celebrate in my own small way working and doing as I would on any Tuesday. Still, I was mindful and observant of the pageantry.

I visited my friend Dianne and helped her hook up her new VCR DVD as she started her day. I watched on her big screen and stayed busy. Dianne has been afflicted with Multiple Sclerosis for more than half her life and is wheelchair-bound. She is a champion of Universal Design, an approach to design that emphasizes access and usability for all, regardless of their physical disability. I half kidded her that this was an inauguration ceremony that was universal by design as we saw the colors of the world and our nation on the screen.

As we watched, I realized that it is how we behave at home and with our neighbors that will dictate how this new era for America will be seen. I pray that we treat each other with kindness and with the freedom, equality and happiness that is our birthright.

As for me, I have a head start. I found a Lincoln penny today. My wishes will be answered closer to home.

Jaye Maynard lives in New York and is a theatrical producer, performer, and customized personal assistant. She collects vintage, plaid, eyewear, and Barbies for fun.

Have A Little Faith

J. Keith Haney

i remember the first time I saw him, election night 2004. I was at the home of a student of mine watching election returns. It looked like W was getting his throne back for another four years. God help us. When that conclusion was confirmed the next day, I wrote a Post-It note at work: "Congratulations, citizens. You've just volunteered for Hell." I complied when I was asked to take that down from my work space, but time still proved me right. I would be lying if I said that I thought it would be this bad.

Barack Obama was the only bright spot of hope on an otherwise hopeless night. I didn't see a lot of him; NBC was cutting between his victory rally in Chicago and the presidential election results. The first person I saw at that rally was Michelle Obama: warm, friendly, but with strength. Then later Obama came out with his family, a strange little hodepodge of folks of various ethnic groups. But that made it seem better to me. If a family like that can exist, maybe there's hope for the world.

I'm not sure exactly when I said this or what made me. But that night, I told my student point-blank, "We're looking at the next President of the United

States." Sounds contrived, doesn't it? More than a little unbelievable? I didn't believe it either, and I said it. For weeks after that, I beat myself up for it. This guy had just gotten elected Senator for the first time, and I was already talking about him being president?! Oh yeah, and he was black. Didn't happen in my parents' lifetime, won't happen in mine. No way.

Then the inexplicable kept happening. The GOP didn't have a single credible candidate that would make everyone happy. Hillary lost to Barack for the nomination. Sarah Palin dragged a weak ticket down to new depths. When McCain melted down with the economy, I knew it was over...just like I'd been told.

In three weeks time, I'm going to see history made for the third time in a row. I have seen an African-American nominated by a major party. I've seen him win. Now I'm going to see him inaugurated. Others are worried about him, but I'm not. Something higher than Man watches over him. It let me see where he was going. The Long Night is finally over. Time for a Brand New Day.

J. Keith Haney, 33, works as an insurance claims processor in Tennessee. Recently, he has taken in an interest in political classics like Machiavelli's The Prince and Sun Tzu's The Art of War.

Not a Dream, a Premonition

Kevin A. Jackson

the day before Barack Obama's inauguration, as we all know, was Martin Luther King Day. As I listened to the "I Have A Dream" speech for the 15th year in a row, the words took on a whole new meaning. The dream MLK had, at that time, had just been a dream. Now that dream is a reality. Children and adults of all races, ages, creeds, and colors work, learn, and play together. And now, thanks to Barack Obama's courage and determination, we can reach new goals.

When I saw the presidential Inauguration and speech, I was in my college's auditorium. The school decided to set up a viewing so the students could watch history be made between classes. I especially needed to be there because I had to write a paper analyzing the speech. As I walked into the auditorium, I felt a bit of dread. Of course, being a young African-American man, I was overjoyed to view the inauguration but I had to do school work as well. It was not until I saw then-President-elect, Barack Obama place his hand on the Bible that I felt it. This was real; this was actually happening! We were seconds away from the President of the United States being an African-American man. I was hit with a wave of emotion as I watched Obama being sworn in, and even laughed at the judge's mistake. Then it was done. My president was black.

As I drove home later that afternoon, the popular song "My President is Black" came on the radio and something extraordinary happened. I wept. I never cry, not even in pain, but the joy I had in my heart was overwhelming. I didn't cry because the president was an African-American, but because he was not Caucasian. The tides had turned in America, and not only Americans knew this but the world. I felt a sense of pride I had never felt before for my country; I felt invincible as if nothing could stop me from following my dreams. Prior to the inauguration, I never felt the way most people felt after the election. But after seeing that oath, I felt the pride and it was strong. From the moment I cried in my car, I swore to myself that I will never let anything hold me back. Not race, not gender, not even myself. I swore that I too will lead a nation.

Kevin A. Jackson, 21, was born in Bronx, New York, but now lives in Georgia where he attends college. He aspires to become an English teacher, author, or editor.

Not Another Tuesday

Amber Payne

When I went to school in weather that was a bit too cold for January in South Carolina, it was a normal Tuesday, or so it seemed. All of the classrooms were freezing as usual. So what made this day any different from any other Tuesday or any other day of the week? Well, today was January 20, Inauguration day, and unlike the last 56 inaugurations, January 20, 2009, was the day Barack Obama was sworn into office.

The strides that Americans have made, not as a nation but as a society ruled by color and status, have been remarkable in the last 60 years. From my grandmother to my father, the opportunities to go further in life have been hard and almost unreachable. Now the dream seems possible and the glass ceiling a hoax.

While Barack Obama spoke, everyone in the schools of Greenville, South Carolina, watched as history wrote in her thick book. For many of us hope was born and hearts stopped in the moment Obama gave his speech.

And as we watch the screen like millions of other people, I listened to my heart beat, the rushing of blood to my legs down to my feet. I listened as words went through one ear and out the other. I listened to the feelings etched through words, through music, through the millions of bodies present. I listened.

I listened not by my ears alone but through my soul, shaky with pride and hope. The future, although cold, worn, and tougher than nails, feels and smells stronger than ever before. We were past slaves, we were Negros that did not belong in American, we were savages that the English came to redeem, we were Indains that "hindered" America's growth. Our sole purpose was to work for the "white man."

But now we are slowly becoming one nation, one people.

Amber Payne, 18, lives in South Carolina, just voted for the first time and sings for fun.

2009: Year of Miracles

Melinda Kucsera

ive days before the inauguration, as an entire world waited, a plane crash-landed in the Hudson River miles from where I live. All the crew and passengers aboard were safely evacuated. Injuries were reported to be minor. That was a miracle, and it happened because the right people were in the right place at the right time. Finally, at the end of 2008, when all hope had been lost in the electoral process and the office of the president in particular, there was the right person for these troubled times.

My grandparents came to this country to escape fascism in Europe a half century ago. They sought a place where they could achieve their dreams, but that wasn't the America they found. What they found was a place less hospitable than where they left, but they kept going: they worked hard and believed in the American dream, even if it didn't always believe in them.

All that changed on Election Day 2008. America's promise of equality to all was validated. America stood proudly as a nation of dreams, and this election was proof that all dreams, no matter their scope or seeming impossibility, do come true. This was the America that every immigrant has searched for and imagined.

One dream, one day, one country cast its ballot and a nation of promise was reborn. This is the time. This is the moment. Dream what you've never dared to; be proud of the great victory our country and its people have accomplished and the drive to persevere no matter the obstacles to our dreams.

This is the year of miracles. One man and his journey to the Oval Office gave a country hope; a plane crashed into a river days before his historic inauguration and no one was harmed. Let these two events stand as two miracles amid a sea of them during this most wonderful time.

God bless America and President Obama, the world, and all its people.

Melinda Kucsera has worked as an editor, writing tutor, designer, website builder, image specialist, and general Photoshop guru, but her passion is photography. She enjoys working out and faithfully chronicling the lives of the characters she invents.

Witnessing a Fourth of the Forty-Four

Brian Barkley

inauguration day is a natural obsession with me. Every four years, my birthday is celebrated with parades and a peaceful transition of power that is almost unique in history. I often wonder how different my life would be if Inauguration Day had remained March 4, as it once was. Would I have still been so interested in history?

When I was a child, I thought it would be great if the day were a national holiday so I could have it off every four years. At my first inauguration in memory, John Kennedy did not interest me. Instead, I ran around the room yelling "I like Ike" whenever the camera flashed on the cold and huddled man who appeared to be withdrawing his head into his shoulders like a turtle. Since then, I always watched every minute of the program and address, no matter how boring it seemed to listen to these old men talk. It is amazing to me how much younger and more interesting they seem now as I watch the replays on C-Span. Even Maya Angelou's "On the Pulse of Morning," is understandable to me now, after having children and aching for them.

I have been a critic of the ceremony, taking note of every change to the setting and program. For someone who takes a personal holiday from work every four years for this ceremony, the mangling of the oath in 2009 was appalling. Had they worn formal morning clothing, the Chief Justice and the president-elect would have sailed through confidently with no problems.

Yet, as President Obama so appropriately quoted from scripture, it is indeed the time to "put away childish things."

The thing that strikes me the most is that simple oath and how each person has interpreted it. The oath for every other federal office is the same, except this one-- prescribed by the Constitution. It's as if our founders used words as alchemy, or an inoculation against pride and corruption for this highest office of the land.

The oath is not important as a rote recitation, but in the character of the person who takes it--what he or she does with it. I have witnessed ten presidents take the same oath, and I have seen how they lived the oath during their terms of office. I am optimistic about the future based on what I perceive about the man who took the oath on January 20, 2009. May God bless him and his endeavors for our country.

Brian Barkley lives in Texas and is the pastor of the First Baptist Church of Edmonston. He works for the state of Texas in health and human services and enjoys British TV, especially the comedies.

Its About Time on 1.20.09 (Barack Obama Gets It).

J-B Hyppolite

It's 12:24 in the morning on Wednesday January 21, 2009. We are 24 minutes into what everyone is calling a new era for America. 1.20.09 was one of the happiest days in American history, period. But why? Everyone has their own reasons. For me, it wasn't just because Barack Obama was sworn in as the first black President of the United States. For this 22-year-old black man, it was witnessing a vision that came to fruition. I can say that I witnessed an America that, for one day, wasn't ruled by racial and cultural differences.

On 1.20.09, that punk-rock black kid didn't have to worry about being called an Oreo by his "own people." That Asian girl didn't have to succumb to stereotypes in order to feel accepted by everyone else. For one moment, we embraced our races, cultures, and everything else to realize what we should have realized all along--that we are Americans and foremost, we are people. We are people not separated and ridiculed for simply being themselves.

It's about time.

It's about time that people realize there is no color in a kiss, no color in love. It's about time that people understand hate and pure ignorance can be erased, if we rise above. It's about time that someone else gets it. On 1.20.09, I saw examples of people unlocking themselves from a prison—a prison of stereotypes, judgments, assumptions, ignorant expectations, and plain-old indifference. Barack Obama always makes sure to mention everyone, acknowledging all the colors and creeds of this country, making sure that while there are differences, they are insignificant. After all, I am him, she is her, and we are all. Barack Obama gets it.

From now on, when I come in contact with the black girl who is told she is too white or the Latino male who gets ridiculed for dating Asian girls, when I see anyone made to feel less because they "don't fit in", I will remind them that there is a man in the highest office that is above such old-fashioned thinking. Luckily for us, Barack Obama gets it.

J-B Hyppolite, 22, hails from Pennsylvania and is a freelance entertainment writer who is working on launching a website entitled Color Blynd Nation. He has been a lyric/songwriter since the age of 13.

The "Yes-We-Can" Man

Nia M. Brown

i am a 34-year-old black woman married to a 45-year-old white man. The 2008 election was the first time either of us had voted in our lives. To some that may seem strange, I know. I guess I figured they would put whomever they wanted in office. However, there was something different about this man with the "Yes We Can" slogan that started pulling at me. I started to wonder, "Can we make a change? Can we make a difference?" And all I kept hearing was "Yes We Can!" My grandparents, who are still both alive, were born during a time when black people where only considered to be three-fifths of a person. I thought about that and what this president could mean not only to me but also my family, and I registered to vote. I also registered my husband. If there was a possibility that our votes really counted, that we could really be heard now was the time to become proactive.

Some may think that we were only doing it because he is black. I had many friends ask me this very question. I won't lie. A good part of it was for that reason alone, but that was not the only reason. I researched this man, his goals, his accomplishments (as well as his shortcomings). It was through my research that I truly started to believe that this was the man who could make a difference.

We cast our votes and waited in anticipation with the rest of the world on November 4, 2008, results. Then: Good heavens!...oh my God!...he won...Obama won! I was speechless, dumbfounded. The "Yes We Can" man won! We had witnessed history. My husband embraced me and said, "See, we can make a difference!" I don't know exactly what role our votes played and I don't know who else voted for him, but I did know that change had come and his name was Obama!

The morning of January 20, 2009, we awoke and sent our 11-year-old son to school. My son is black. Before he left home I reminded him of something I had told him millions of times over, "You can be anything you want to be!" But this time I added "Including president!" When my husband returned from taking him to school, we watched again in anticipation, but this time we were waiting for him to take the presidential oath. As I looked on from home, my eyes started to fill with tears, and I could feel my heart start to swell. I could hear angels. I imagined them rejoicing with songs of praise. Then, with his right hand raised and his left atop a bible, he was officially sworn into office.

Nothing can erase the hurt and pain that has taken place in our history. But it is just that—"PAST HISTORY!" The beauty of January 20, 2009, is something that will live on in our nation's history forever. Before the question was: "Can we?" The answer was: "Yes we can!" With the swearing in of Barack Obama as our 44th President, we now can say: "Yes we did!" God bless our nation. We can, and we will overcome!

Nia M. Brown, 34, a graduate of the Art Institute of Pittsburgh, lives in Washington state and works as a freelance designer and colorist.

With Love, From England

Kerry Bird

the word "Obama" meant nothing to me, a 13-year-old grammar school girl from England, until late summer of 2008. I took little interest in him at first.

As election night grew closer, people around the world starting taking interest, myself included. "Is the USA ready for a black president?" we asked ourselves. Surely not. And then, on November 4, 2008, America proved to the world that they were ready.

Their first black president had been elected. Nothing else was shown on the news that night, apart from ecstatic supporters and disappointed opposition. When we heard his victory speech, heard everything he stood for, we knew America had gotten it right.

All of a sudden, Obama was the topic of conversation everywhere. He was praised and disliked in equal measures at first, before people realized just what this signified. Equality was no longer the dream of a few select individuals. Today, the world's most powerful nation has accepted it with open arms, ready to begin a new page of Earth's history.

If anyone out there is watching us and our planet, perhaps they've now realized that there is hope for us yet. It has taken us thousands of years, but we've finally overcome one huge hurdle in the race for equality.

You did it, America. Congratulations. I salute you; you've shown everyone exactly what you can do. And to President Obama: Good luck. I pray that the rest of the world is right behind you on this one—you are much more than "just another president" to many people around the globe.

Kerry Bird is a teenager from the UK who enjoys reading, writing, and horse riding.

With a Name Comes Change

Cristin Marie Kennedy

With a name like Kennedy, one would think I'd be interested in politics. I'm not. I think politics is a dirty game full of lies, backstabbing, name-calling, and popularity contests. I've never been sucked into any presidential candidate or campaign. Until now.

Until this election I didn't watch campaign commercials or debates on TV. I likewise stopped watching the news a while back when I lost pride in my country. I wasn't proud of neighbors who weren't friendly, criminals in our cities, "dirty" police officers and lawyers who let convicts off, the justice system's lack of fairness, or the unaccountability of those in highest positions.

When a woman and an African-American man both announced they would be running for president in the Democratic primaries, I decided to have faith in my country again. I stopped looking at the campaign as "politics" and started looking at it as "American rights". I started having hope in the American people. Maybe we could stop living in the past, and move toward a better future. I remembered my own childhood saying, "I want to be the first woman president!"

This year was the first time I voted. It was a day that could change my future, my children's future, the future of our country, and the future of the world. I felt part of history in the making. My own textbooks recall the inauguration of John F. Kennedy, and I have heard my elders' stories remembering that day. Now I can tell my children and grandchildren, "I was there. I remember..."

The inauguration of President Barack H. Obama is an historical one. The ballot I filled out had a bubble filled with his name next to it. I have high hopes for our country with him as our leader. The world will see that Americans' views have changed. We have compassion toward fellow people—not just one race or religion, and we want to see a *global* change.

It will be a painstaking, long, upward battle, but change can be achieved. Our president holds a heavy burden now, but I have faith he will hold it high and with dignity and strength. Our Leader needs our help to bring this to fruition. Let us help him achieve this seemingly impossible feat.

Cristin Marie Kennedy, 24, is a stay-at-home mom of two daughters, ages four and one. She lives in a suburb of Orlando, Florida and is an amateur photographer who enjoys singing karaoke in her spare time.

One Man, One Nation, One World

Vanessa Cobb

the crystal blue morning bode well for a day to remember. Some 3500 miles to the west, the president-elect would be sleeping still—or perhaps not.

I hadn't given it much thought. Stopping at the corner shop, I overheard a conversation between shoppers. One said she had a dental appointment that would clash with the ceremony. The other nodded absently, as if her friend had been referring to a grading at the Judo club. I glanced at the front page of my newspaper and smiled.

As I walked back to my home office, the air felt alive with static. Crackles of curiosity were sparking from a remote frequency. Before long I was absorbed in paperwork, and eight hours later my working day was done. It was 5 p.m. in the UK, and within the next thirty minutes the most consequential promise of the century was to be pledged.

I almost missed it. I flicked on the TV hoping to find some light entertainment. Fortunately, proceedings had been delayed.

The Quaker hymn underscoring John Williams' composition "Air and Simple Gifts" conveyed the same restraint and dignity that unfolded from Obama's words, with more talk of peace and courage than needless protestations for democracy and integrity.

The image of his two-mile audience will never leave me. The power of their silent attention and collective will, focused upon a single slice of history, transformed a rallying speech into a contract. While Obama spoke of hope, his confidence declared nothing less than conviction: these things shall be. Here is a leader everyone can believe in; not just because we like him, not just because he's different and breaks tradition from the privilege of race, but because he has made up his mind.

He was speaking to me, as much as to anyone. Here, in my Devon living room, the forty-fourth President of the United States of America was calling me to action.

It's tempting to envy Americans the experience of Obama's elevation. Yet none of us will be far removed from its influence. Obama has managed in one statement to affirm his authenticity, to unite his country and to embrace his world. He is the iconic Millennium Leader—at once an architect of global change and a bloke you would want to add as a friend on Facebook.

Rather like the shadow-less warning of Groundhog Day, however, we know that both the weather and state of the world's wealth could remain icy for some time, and one of them perhaps long into Obama's first term. I'm not expecting a miracle; I'm expecting hard work. But many hands will make light of it. If he's done nothing else already, Barack Obama has extended a refreshing spirit of brotherhood to every corner of the planet. As for this fellow citizen of the world, count me in.

Vanessa Cobb lives in a market town in Devon, UK, with her sixteen-year-old son. She runs a small management training and coaching business, but is striving to become a full-time writer. Her first novel, The Colour Caster, is due to be published by WEbook in 2009.

What is WEbook?

WEbook.com is an online community where writers, readers, and "feedbackers" create great books and cast their votes to make their favorite undiscovered writers the next published authors.

WEbook is an innovative avenue for new writers to find an audience. WEbook.com satisfies the dreams of millions of aspiring authors and taps the wisdom of the crowd to create a unique new form of creative work: community-sourced books.

Jan 20 2009 is WEbook's first Community-Sourced History. This book—comprising 60 select essays from 58 writers—was sourced from hundreds of essays on WEbook.com from writers across the globe. Because of its huge community, worldwide reach, and web-enabled writing platform, WEbook is uniquely well-positioned to create and publish nearly "instant books" related to major current events.

WEbook's other titles include *Pandora* and *101 Things Every Man Should Know How to Do*. Upcoming titles include *The Legend of Vinny Whiskers*, *The Color Caster*, and *Expat Journal*.

WEbook.com is a whole new way of looking at how books are written and picked for publication. Learn more and see how you can be part of the revolution at www.WEbook.com.

Made in the USA
Monee, IL
08 July 2026

56644837R00085